PUBLISHING
IN
MAINLAND CHINA

M.I.T. REPORT NUMBER 4

PUBLISHING
IN
MAINLAND CHINA

G. Raymond Nunn

THE M.I.T. PRESS

Massachusetts Institute of Technology
Cambridge, Massachusetts, and London, England

This study attempts to analyze the organization of book and periodical publishing in China from 1949 to the end of 1964, with particular reference to publications in the natural, applied, and social sciences. Publishing is a small industry in all countries. The relative monetary value of its total output is small. It employs few people. In China, out of a total population of over 600 million, probably not more than 45,000 were employed in all phases of the industry (including distribution) at its height.

In spite of its small size, the publishing industry plays a vital role in the communication of knowledge. The impact of publishing is selective in affecting a relatively small but influential sector of the population. In China, where the output and subject matter of books and periodicals are carefully controlled, what is published is a most valuable indicator of government policy. Further, for a developing country like China, the communication role is even more critical in that publishing transmits from the rest of the world the scientific and technical information essential for continued growth.

Sources for the study of contemporary publishing in any country are restricted and meager. For this study one principal source has been accounts of the publishing industry brought together and placed on microfilm by the Union Research Institute in Hong Kong and the various series of translated materials published by the United States Consulate General in Hong Kong and by the Joint Publications Research Series. A second and independent source has been found in the two major national bibliographies developed in China. These are the Ch'üan kuo hsin shu mu, or National Catalogue of New Books, which has been published from 1950 to the present, and the Ch'üan kuo ts'ung shu mu, or National Cumulative Catalogue of Books, an annual cumulation listing publications issued from 1949 through 1958. Through analysis of the items listed in these two catalogues, a great deal of information has been derived regarding the structure of the industry, the size of publishing houses, the relative amounts of literature published in minority and foreign languages, and the relative amounts published by subject. The two catalogues have an added advantage in that they may be considered to have the necessary accuracy of a telephone directory, and they have provided a very valuable check for statements published in newspapers and periodicals.

The analysis has been limited by the data which are available. It needs to be completed by a physical-site visit and access to internal trade documentation, without which a full understanding of the processes through which scientific and other information is circulated in China is impossible. Such a field study is not feasible under present conditions.

I would like to take this opportunity to acknowledge the encouragement of Dr. Burton Adkinson and Dr. Arthur Shanahan of the National Science Foundation, and the continuous assistance of Mr. Kay Kitagawa, formerly of the Office of Foreign Science Information in the Foundation. The National Science Foundation provided the financial support which made this study possible. My colleagues on the Association for Asian Studies' Committee on American Library Resources for the Far East (CALRFE) have assisted in every way possible in the provision of data for the preliminary studies in this project. The Association's Secretary, Dr. L.A. Peter Gosling, and its Office Manager, Mrs. Victoria Harper, have provided valuable administrative support, enabling me to concentrate on the preparation of the reports that have come out of the study. Neither the National Science Foundation nor the Association for Asian Studies is responsible for the views expressed in these reports. Among the many who have assisted considerably in the study I would like to mention Dr. Susan Han Marsh, Mr. Thomas Gregory Song, Mr. William C. C. Hu, and Mr. Douglas Tann, all of whom have spent long hours in the compilation of the statistical and other data employed in the study.

Honolulu
November 1965

G. Raymond Nunn

CONTENTS

LIST OF TABLES

CHAPTER 1

FLOW OF INFORMATION FROM OUTSIDE CHINA AND ITS DEVELOPMENT IN CHINA

China faces the problem, common to all major countries, of keeping abreast of world developments in all fields of knowledge. Furthermore, it finds itself at a disadvantage, along with such other non-Western-European countries as Japan and the Soviet Union, in that the great part of the information it requires is written in English. This disadvantage has been met in a number of ways. In the first place, foreign currency allocations have been made for centralized purchase through Peking of printed materials from the Soviet Union and other countries. This purchase program is supplemented by a system of exchange, again centralized, in this case through the National Library of Peking and the Institute of Scientific and Technical Information, a division of the Chinese Academy of Sciences. Soviet documentation has become a principal implement for developing China. Russian has replaced English as the language of higher education, permitting direct use of the large volume of Soviet materials that have been acquired.

Purchase of Materials

The principal channel through which information flows into China is through the direct purchase of materials by agents of the Guozi Shudian (International Bookstore) abroad. From 1950 to 1953 the Guozi Shudian imported 47 million books and exported 8 million.[1] A very substantial proportion of the imported books were from the Soviet Union. For the eighteen-month period from January 1950 through June 1951 alone, 9,365,844 volumes, 2,606,847 issues of periodicals, and 1,521,915 maps and phonograph records were imported from the Soviet Union.[2] In 1959 the Library of the Chinese Academy of Sciences subscribed to 527 Russian periodicals.[3]

Although the Guozi Shudian is solely responsible for the import of foreign-language materials, it shares the responsibility for internal distribution of foreign periodicals with the Hsin Hua Shu Tien (New China Book Company). A principal expansion took place in 1956, when the distribution of foreign-language periodicals, which previously had been limited to 90 branches of the Guozi Shudian and the Hsin Hua Shu Tien, was expanded to include post offices in 190 large and medium-sized cities. The number of different titles handled was expanded from 800 in 1955 to 1,037 in 1956.[4] In 1956, the foreign-language periodical catalogue issued by the Guozi Shudian listed 3,000 periodicals, but some of these were annual reports and reports on the internal affairs of societies.[5]

At a meeting convened by the import department of the Guozi Shudian in May 1957 there was criticism of the distribution arrangements for imported books and periodicals. One scientist considered that these materials should be imported at a number of places rather than through one central office and that the Guozi Shudian should undertake both importing and distribution instead of distributing through the Hsin Hua Shu Tien. Another scientist was critical of the £400,000 appropriation for the import of scientific books and periodicals for 1958. He considered this insufficient, claiming that £1,500,000 would not be too much.[6]

Owing to the limited amount of foreign currency, it was inevitable that criticism would be leveled at purchases of foreign periodicals, particularly at the wastes due to poor selection on the part of purchasers.[7] For example, in 1956 the different departments of the College of Science at Wuhan University purchased 285 periodicals from outside the Communist bloc, and 42 of these titles were found to be duplicates.[8]

Japan has also emerged as a source of supply of scientific literature. A special service for the abstracting of Japanese articles in scientific periodicals commenced in 1963. Currently, scientific books are being purchased in Japan and imported through Hong Kong in lots of 50 copies per title. The fields in which China has expressed an interest are medicine, chemistry, engineering, and electrical engineering. Both current and older materials have been purchased.[9]

Exchange of Materials

In much the same way that the import of purchased materials is centralized through the Guozi Shudian, the import of materials received through
international library exchange is centralized through the National Library of
Peking and the Institute of Scientific and Technical Information of China of
the Chinese Academy of Sciences. In addition to maintaining major exchange
relations since early 1958, the National Library has been the center for interlibrary borrowing from Soviet libraries and for the supply of microfilm of
materials in Soviet libraries. [10]

As can be seen from Table 1, the volume of materials sent out of China
by the National Library of Peking rose to a peak of 170,000 books in 1958 and
fell off to 135,000 books and periodicals in 1961. The number of countries
with which the National Library exchanged, as well as the number of books
and periodicals received, continued to increase; in both cases, the 1961 figures exceeded those of 1958.

A high proportion of the exchanges has been conducted with the Soviet
Union. From 1949 to 1959, 290,000 books and periodicals were received
from the Soviet Union, and 306,000 books and periodicals were sent in exchange. In 1958 the National Library was exchanging directly with 98 public
libraries, colleges, museums, institutes, and publishing houses in the Soviet
Union. [11]

This major exchange relationship with the Soviet Union has had its effect
on the holdings of the National Library. Its Soviet book and periodical holdings
increased from 4,000 in 1949 to 240,000 in 1959, and over two-thirds of the
latter number were received through exchange. Since altogether 306,000
books and periodicals were received in exchange, there is a balance of about
146,000 pieces which were sent to other Chinese libraries. [12]

China has maintained close exchange relations with other Communist
bloc countries. Under the Sino-Korean Economic and Cultural Agreement,
170,000 books and periodicals were sent to North Korea, and over 50,000
books and periodicals received in return. [13] The National Library also sent
4,700 books and periodicals to the Berlin State Library and to other libraries
in East Germany and received 6,600 books and periodicals in exchange.
Materials received by the National Library were principally scientific periodicals. [14]

Table 1. Publication Exchanges by the National Library
of Peking, 1949-1961

Year	Materials Sent	Materials Received	Number of Countries and Areas Conducting Exchanges
1949-1953	30,000 books	50,000 books	18
1954	110,000 books and periodicals	30,000 books	37
1958	170,000 books	87,000 books	Over 100
1961	135,000 books and periodicals	110,000 books and periodicals	160

Sources:

1949-1953   Peking New China News Agency (NCNA) Dec. 27, 1953, translated in Survey of China Mainland Press (SCMP) 716, p. 11.

1954   Peking NCNA Jan. 13, 1955, translated in SCMP 968, p. 3

1958   Peking NCNA English Sept. 4, 1959, in SCMP 2004, p. 16.

1961   Peking NCNA English, Aug. 7, 1961, in SCMP 2557, p. 19.

Note: The term "books" appears to have been used as though it were interchangeable with "books and periodicals." Probably both expressions refer to "pieces," used indiscriminately to refer to both issues of periodicals and volumes of books.

The principal other institution in China maintaining foreign exchange relations is the Chinese Academy of Sciences, through its Institute of Scientific and Technical Information of China. In 1955, 157,000 books and periodicals were received, and 39,300 were sent. Exchange relations were developed with 733 different bodies in 51 countries. [15] These exchange arrangements were made on behalf of the research institutes of the Academy of Sciences for the acquisition of materials which could not be obtained by subscription. One of the most important acquisitions of the Academy has been a complete card index of articles in Soviet periodicals published since the second half of 1955, which was sent by the All-Union State Library of Foreign Literature. [16] The Academy

Library received three gift shipments from the Soviet Union. The June 1955 shipment included 67,000 volumes.[17]

What do the National Library of Peking and the Chinese Academy of Sciences have to offer in exchange? In the first place, the National Library has access to metropolitan publishing and warehousing sources superior to those available to the market in Hong Kong, the principal location for the purchase of Chinese publications. Second, it is able to carry stocks of publications that have become exhausted in Hong Kong. Third, it is able to offer materials, particularly periodicals, that are not available through the Hong Kong market. The Chinese Academy of Sciences offers scientific periodicals that are not available through the Hong Kong dealers. All these materials are in Chinese; to develop exchange potential among libraries without Chinese collections, it proved necessary to provide English-language periodicals. Science Record, Scientia Sinica, and the Chinese Medical Journal have filled this role. An addition to this limited list was provided by the Science Abstracts of China, which were published in 1958 and 1959 and resumed publication again in 1963. These abstracts reported current Chinese scientific research. In the first 1963 issue of each of the six sections of the abstracts there appeared an invitation for "all academic societies, research institutes, colleges, universities and scientific concerns of foreign countries ... to use their own publications for exchange."

The advantages of these exchange arrangements can be seen in the example of one American university library which in 1963 purchased all 43 Chinese-language periodicals available for subscription through the Hong Kong dealers and obtained on exchange an additional 30 periodicals distributed in China but not available in Hong Kong for subscription. The latter group included 15 periodicals from the natural and applied sciences.

Many major university libraries in the United States were compelled to enter into exchanges to obtain materials not available for subscription in Hong Kong after the severe restrictions on the export of periodicals went into effect in September 1959. This situation has been carefully exploited by the National Library, which has transformed many of these libraries, through their exchange operations, into its acquisition agencies, particularly with respect to materials that are difficult to acquire through the book trade.

précis this

Abstracting and Control of Foreign Scientific Literature

We have already referred to the role of the Institute of Scientific and Technical Information of China in the acquisition of materials on exchange. This Institute is the principal body responsible for documentation of foreign scientific developments. In the field of publication, one of its first ventures was the issue of a new journal, K'o hsüeh hsin wen (Science News), in 1955. At first this journal reported only foreign scientific and technical information, but later it began to report Chinese developments as well. [18]

The vast field of foreign scientific information was being controlled in the early 1960's by an index to articles published in foreign scientific and technical periodicals. This index was issued in 28 monthly parts, and it surveyed over 7,000 periodicals in a wide range of languages, selecting from them over 15,000 articles for listing. [19]

The Annotated List of Scientific and Technical Periodicals, 1961 was published by the Institute in 1961. It lists 15 abstracting journals or series of abstracts. A large number of these were noted among the exchange materials being received by the National Diet Library in Tokyo at the end of 1963. Nearly all of these abstracting journals are translated from their Russian counterparts. They show a preponderance of abstracts of English-language articles, followed by articles in Russian, with Japanese articles a poor third. Since 1963 the Institute has also published a special Abstracts of Articles Published in Japanese Scientific and Technical Periodicals. It is planned to include 200 abstracts in each issue.

Abstracting and translation journals represent a very high proportion of the total volume of Chinese scientific periodicals reaching libraries outside the Communist bloc. As much as 15 per cent of the total number of periodical titles examined fell into this category, about half being devoted to translation and half to abstracting. In the Annotated List mentioned above, there are 13 "express" reports listed, and these contain articles that have been translated into Chinese, edited, and published by the Institute. In addition to these translation sources, many of the standard scientific journals contain translated articles, particularly from the Russian literature.

Organization of Translation

One of the first difficulties faced by the Chinese in the early fifties arose from the small number of persons able to translate from Russian. A study made in June 1952 showed that there were only 600 persons so qualified. [20] Training of Russian-language students commenced, and in 1957 alone it was reported that there were 3,000 Russian-language graduates, a number in excess of needs. [21] In the meantime, there was a major task of translation to be done, and under a directive of November 1952 the Ministry of Higher Education organized faculty members in universities and colleges and provided for the translation of scientific, industrial, and agricultural textbooks and reference books amounting to 67 million words. [22]

The First National Translation Work Conference was opened by the Publications Administrative Bureau in November 1951. The conference provided for the standardization of translated terms and the compilation of dictionaries and glossaries. It revised the list of books for translation in 1952 and ratified draft regulations for translating and for the publication of translations. [23] Translators were associated with publishing houses in very much the same way that writers are, and the publishing houses were charged with the specific duty of translation. All the translation journals that appeared before 1959 were issued by the various specialist publishing houses, not by a central agency. The publishing houses tend to favor veteran translators with whom they are familiar. Both the translators and the houses tend to favor books that are likely to be popular and secure greater sales and more profit. These tendencies result in a shortage of translations of academic work. [24]

In 1956 the Chinese Academy of Sciences set up its Translation and Publication Committee to determine policy for scientific publications and to examine and approve plans for scientific publishing. The Committee was also charged with providing standard terms for translation. [25] A similar meeting was held in December 1957 to discuss objectives for 1958. The publishing plan of the Science Press (a unit of the Academy), the number of titles, the proportion of translation and original work, the number of glossaries, and the proportion of books to be published in each scientific field covered by the plan were studied. [26]

Volume of Translation

From the Handbook on People's China we learn that from October 1949 to the end of 1955, 12,157 foreign works were translated. An earlier source states that up to May 1955, 10,000 books had been translated, and that 8,400 of these were Russian books.[27] Table 2 shows the division of these translations by broad subject class.

Table 2. Translations Published in China, October 1949 to May 1955

Subject Area	Russian Books	Books in Other Languages	Total
Works of Marx, Engels, Lenin, and Stalin	209	-	209
Social sciences	1900	100	2000
Natural and applied sciences	2400	1000	3400
Foreign literature, art, and other books	3900	500	4400
Total	8409	1600	10009

Source: Jen min jih pao (People's Daily), Aug. 30, 1955, translated in SCMP 1136, pp. 23-24.

Table 3 shows a considerable decline in the percentage of Russian-language books translated and published from 1954 through 1964. It is interesting to note that the percentage of titles translated from other languages has remained fairly constant. After Russian, English publications constitute the next largest group translated, ranging from 1 to 1.5 per cent of the total number of titles published, with American books somewhat more heavily represented than British.

One of the striking features of publishing in China since 1949 has been the broadcasting of the classics of Communism. Up to the end of 1960, over

Table 3. *Percentage of Book Publication Translated from Russian and Other Languages, 1954-1964*

Year	From Russian	From other languages
1954	45%	6%
1955	46	5
1956	38	5
1957	38	5
1958	17	3
1959 (Estimate)	11	4
1960 (Estimate)	7	3
1962 (Estimate)	6	4
1963	7	3
1964 (Estimate)	7	4

Sources: Ch'üan kuo ts'ung shu mu (National Cumulative Catalogue of Books) for materials published from 1954 through 1958, and Ch'üan kuo hsin shu mu (National Catalogue of New Books) for 1959, 1960, 1962 through 1964.

300 books by Marx, Engels, Lenin, and Stalin had been published, in over 50 million copies.[28] About one-third of these were the works of Stalin. In addition to being translated and published in China, copies of Stalin's works in Chinese translation were imported from the Foreign Languages Publishing House in Moscow. By 1954 nearly four million copies had been imported.[29] At the same time, over three million copies of Lenin's works were imported and distributed in China.[30]

Another large group of materials translated from Russian has been literary works. Initially, this group was better represented than books in the natural and applied sciences. However, in the long run, the principal interest has been in translation of materials in the applied sciences. In 1953 the Ministry of Higher Education organized the translation of Soviet textbooks for institutions of higher education and secondary technical schools. Over 60 per cent were in the field of engineering.

TABLE 4. *Books Translated into Chinese from*
Russian and Other Languages in 1964

Subject Area	Russian Language	Other Languages
Works of Marx, Engels, Lenin, and Stalin	22	14
International Communist movement	2	10
Communist movement, party, party construction	2	4
Philosophy	4	8
History	2	4
Economics	8	–
Politics and social life	2	4
Culture and education	–	2
Language	–	2
Literature	4	6
Arts	4	16
Religion and atheism	–	2
Science	40	38
Geology and geography	10	2
Biology	8	10
Medicine	10	2
Agriculture	–	4
	118	128
Industry		
– Standards	–	4
	6	–
– Power machinery	4	10
– Electrical machinery, radio, automation	72	32
– Mining	10	4
– Metallurgy, mechanical engineering	74	14
– Light industry, handicrafts	8	4
– Chemical engineering	22	8
– Construction	24	2
– Highway engineering	30	2
	250	80
Total	368	208

Sources: Ch'üan kuo hsin shu mu, issues 6-11, 13-16, 20, and 22 for 1964.
Figures have been doubled to estimate the annual number of translations.

Table 4 shows this same emphasis in 1964. In nearly all fields there was a relative balance between materials translated from Russian and from all other languages, but in the field of engineering Russian materials provided three times as many translation sources as all other languages. Materials published in engineering represented nearly 60 per cent of the total number of translations published in 1964.

The Author

We have so far discussed the flow of information from outside China; we will now turn to its generation within China. Here the principal role is played by the author. Ideally, close relations between author and publisher make it desirable for authors to be located near the main publishing centers. In China, existence of such a situation was partially confirmed by a statement in the Shanghai Wen hui pao (Wen hui Daily) that the number of writers attached to publishing houses in Shanghai increased from 3,050 in 1957 to 5,870 in 1958.[32] Since 1958 the relative strength of local publishing houses outside the main centers of Peking and Shanghai has grown considerably, and we may eventually expect a more even distribution of authors throughout China.

A great deal of attention has been paid in China to the problem of securing new writers. Many of the additional writers noted in Shanghai in 1958 were new writers. The problem of locating and utilizing new writers is of course not restricted to the Chinese publishing industry. Established writers are known to readers, and their books will naturally sell better. The newly discovered writer usually presents such problems as an inability to properly organize a manuscript.[33] Nevertheless, the National Conference on Publication Work held in 1958 proposed that 10 per cent of the books published each year should be by new writers.[34]

The system used for the payment of authors is not clear. In one case, the well-known writer Pa Chin was criticized for the large payments he received for his book Living Among Heroes. Seventy thousand copies of this book were printed and sold at 3,200 yuan a copy. Pa Chin received royalties of 33,600,000 yuan, or 15 per cent of the total sales. He received 24,000,000 yuan from the sales of his book Tales of the Heroes.[35] The established rates of payment to authors were later considered excessive. In 1958 the leading publishing houses in Shanghai reduced their payments for articles in periodicals and newspapers and for books, and the houses in Peking followed their lead. The general rate for payment was cut in half, both for original writing and for translation.[36]

Professional writers are organized in the Chinese Union of Writers. Not all writers are so organized. From one source we read of 530 professional writers submitting their plans for original writing for 1956 to the Chinese Union of Writers. This number is a small proportion of the total number of writers in China if the above account of the total number of writers attached to Shanghai publishing houses in 1957 is correct. The writing plans of these 530 authors were exclusively literary.[37] In the field of children's literature, there were 60 writers who were members of the Chinese Union of Writers. In addition, there were 700 amateur writers.[38]

References

1. Peking New China News Agency (NCNA) July 30, 1954, translated in Survey of China Mainland Press (SCMP).

2. Jen min jih pao, Feb. 14, 1952, translated in SCMP 294, p. 26.

3. Rafikov, A. "In Chinese Libraries." Special Libraries, vol. 51, no. 10, Dec. 1960, p. 528.

4. Peking NCNA Aug. 24, 1956, translated in SCMP 1363, p. 11.

5. Jen min jih pao, Sept. 1, 1956, translated in SCMP 1385, p. 7.

6. Jen min jih pao, June 3, 1957, translated in SCMP 1562, p. 4.

7. Jen min jih pao, Sept. 1, 1956, translated in SCMP 1385, p. 51.

8. Ma, John T. "Chung kuo ta lu t'u shu kuan chin shih ts'a lu." (Notes on recent developments of libraries in mainland China) Hai wai lun t'an (World Forum), vol. 2, no. 5 and no. 6, June and July 1961, p. 7.

9. Source: a leading publisher in Tokyo.

10. Peking NCNA English Sept. 11, 1959, in SCMP 2098, p. 6.

11. Ibid.

12. Ibid.

13. Pyongyang NCNA Nov. 23, 1954, translated in SCMP 935, p. 18.

14. Peking NCNA Dec. 14, 1955, translated in SCMP 1191, p. 24.

15. Peking Kuang ming jih pao (Enlightenment Daily), Oct. 6, 1956, translated in SCMP 1401, p. 7.

16. Ibid., p. 9.

17. Ibid., p. 8.

References (Continued)

18. U.S. Library of Congress. Air Information Division, Library Services Division. List of Communist Chinese Scientific and Technical Periodicals, 1961, p. 25.

19. Figures compiled from Chinese Academy of Sciences, Annotated List of Scientific and Technical Periodicals, 1961.

20. Peking NCNA Dec. 24, 1952, translated in SCMP 481, p. 5.

21. Orleans, Leo A. Professional manpower and education in Communist China. Washington, National Science Foundation, 1961, p. 94.

22. Peking NCNA May 25, 1953, translated in SCMP 578, p. 5.

23. Peking NCNA Nov. 26, 1951, translated in SCMP 222, pp. 8-9.

24. Jen min jih pao, Aug. 30, 1955, translated in SCMP 1136, p. 25.

25. Peking NCNA May 19, 1956, translated in SCMP 1304, pp. 11-12.

26. Peking Kuang ming jih pao, Dec. 28, 1957, translated in SCMP 1691, p. 3.

27. Jen min jih pao, Aug. 30, 1955, translated in SCMP 1136, p. 23.

28. Peking NCNA English Nov. 8, 1960, in SCMP 2378, p. 27.

29. Peking NCNA March 5, 1954, translated in SCMP 761, p. 14.

30. Peking NCNA Jan. 21, 1954, translated in SCMP 734, p. 23.

31. Peking Kuang ming jih pao, Jan. 25, 1954, translated in SCMP 749, p. 14.

32. Shanghai Wen hui pao, Feb. 2, 1959, translated in SCMP 1962, p. 9.

33. Peking Kuang ming jih pao, Nov. 3, 1955, translated in SCMP 1198, pp. 13-15.

34. Shanghai NCNA English March 18, 1958, in SCMP 1737, p. 18.

35. Hong Kong Hsin tao wan pao (Hong Kong Evening News), March 8, 1954, translated in SCMP 763, p. 33.

36. Peking NCNA Sept. 30, 1958, translated in SCMP 1875, pp. 4-5.

37. Peking NCNA Feb. 27, 1956, translated in SCMP 1248, p. 16.

38. Peking NCNA English Aug. 5, 1960, in SCMP 2315, p. 25.

CHAPTER 2

PUBLISHING OF BOOKS AND PERIODICALS

Organization of Publishing

We will now turn from the process of generation of translated and original manuscripts to the mechanism that makes possible their distribution throughout China: the Chinese publishing house.

Until the end of 1950 the major Chinese publishing houses were almost self-sufficient economic units, organizing their own printing, publishing, and distributing through their own outlets. This unity of function was called the "three-in-one" system in Chinese publishing. Such companies were the Commercial Press, which had been established in 1897, and the Chung Hua Book Company, established in 1912. The Communist-controlled Hsin Hua Shu Tien, which was state-owned, followed the same pattern, and had 887 branches and 30 printing plants.[1] However, by 1950, a bureau of the Ministry of Culture, the Publications Administrative Bureau, which had been established to control publishing, began to develop control over such subsidiary operations as printing and distribution, which had previously been the domain of the publishing houses.

The first National Conference on Publications was held by the Publications Administrative Bureau in September 1950. At the conference it was established that the Bureau was to be concerned with policy and with supervising the execution of policy by the publishing houses. The publishing industry was to become more specialized. The functions of printing, publishing proper, and distribution were to be separated. In addition to being restricted to the function of publishing proper, the individual houses were to have their own subject fields.[2]

The first National Publications Administration Conference was held in August and September 1951. It was convened by the Publications Administrative Bureau and was attended by delegates from the Bureau, the Hsin Hua Shu Tien, the Hsin Hua Printing Press, and the publications agencies of the central and local governments. Delegates were asked to draw up publication plans and were urged to publish books in economics and science.[3] At the conference, the Provisional Regulations Governing the Control of Book and

Periodical Publishing (Appendix A) and the Provisional Measures Governing the Registration of Periodicals (Appendix B) were promulgated.

These regulations provided for the registration of publishing, printing, and distributing houses. Publishing houses were required to specialize (presumably by subject area), to submit publication plans to the local publications administration, and to send sample copies of their books and periodicals to the publications administration and to state libraries. One copy each of books and periodicals was to be sent to the local publications administration before distribution.

Completion of the specialization process separating publishing, printing, and distribution in the publishing industry was announced by Hu Yu-chih, director of the Publications Administrative Bureau, at the second National Publications Conference, held in October 1952. Hu considered the chief problems of the industry to be the duplication of subjects — when many needed titles were not in print — and the overstocking of books in some areas along with shortages in others.[4]

TABLE 5. *Number of Local and National Publishing Houses, 1954-1964*

Year	Local Houses	National Houses	Total
1954	30	68	98
1955	24	74	98
1956	25	72	97
1957	29	74	103
1958	27	77	104
1959 (Estimate)	25	62	87
1960 (Estimate)	34	66	100
1962 (Estimate)	27	54	81
1963	28	51	79
1964 (Estimate)	35	47	82

Sources: Ch'üan kuo ts'ung shu mu and Ch'üan kuo hsin shu mu.

Table 5 shows the number of publishing houses each year and changes in their location since 1954. The number of national houses has decreased, while the number of local houses has remained fairly constant, thereby improving the relative strength of the local houses as a group.

The second major change that has taken place in the industry has been the elimination of a large number of houses and the transformation of private and joint state-private houses into state-owned houses. In 1950 there was only one state-owned house, while there were 6 jointly owned houses, and 244 private houses.[5] By 1954 the number of private houses had dropped to 97,[6] by 1956 to 20,[7] and in October 1957, the Jen min jih pao was able to announce the complete elimination of private houses in the industry.

The simple statement that there were 97 publishing houses in 1956 is not too significant unless we can group these houses by size. To do this, the gross income of each house was estimated by constructing a sample from the editions of the Ch'üan kuo ts'ung shu mu published from 1954 to 1957. The total number of copies of each title published was multiplied by the price in order to determine the amount of income from each book. Then the income from all titles published was added for each firm. In this way, the gross income for each firm was estimated.

The data show that over half of the publication output for the period 1954 to 1957 was issued by seven large houses. These were the People's Press, which was responsible for one-fifth of the total, the People's Education Press, the Cartographic Press, the People's Health Press, the Higher Education Press, the Engineering Industry Press, and the China Youth Press. At the other end of the scale, over half of the houses published less than 6 per cent of the national gross output by value of publications. For the period from 1958 to 1964 the trend has been for the output to be less concentrated among a few houses. However, taking the output of these years as a whole, the 20 largest publishing houses were responsible for a substantial proportion of the total publishing output.

The National Conference for Promotion of a Leap Forward in Publishing Work met in March 1958 in Shanghai. The conference called for an increase in the work of the local publishing houses. It was already clear from the January 1958 issues of the Ch'üan kuo hsin shu mu that the local publishing houses, many of which were in the lowest output group in 1956 or were simply not active at all,

were beginning to grow. In the period from 1958 to 1964, 8 of the 20 largest
houses were local ones.

In spite of the policy of subject specialization, wasteful duplication of
subjects continued. In 1956, the Peking Ta kung pao (L'Impartiale) reported
that 50 books on hog breeding had been published by 27 publishing houses, and
39 books had been published on the setting up of rural clubs. [8]

Control of what is published appears to be a matter of self-discipline in
the industry. The formal prohibitions are outlined in regulations, and the de-
posit of copies of published works before distribution provides against a press's
publishing materials that are inimical to the interests of the Chinese Communist authorities. Initially, the situation was brought under control by the mass
destruction of stocks held over from before October 1949. For example, the
Commercial Press had 8,000 items in stock in the summer of 1950; by November 1951 the stock had been examined, and only 1,234 items were permitted to
be distributed. From the Chung Hua Book Company stock of 13,000 items,
only 2,000 were permitted to be circulated. The remainder was sold as
wastepaper. [9]

The strong control over publishing exercised by the Chinese Communist
authorities was shown by the denunciation in 1957 of Tseng Yen-hsiu, director
of the People's Press. Tseng, it was claimed, was opposed to planning for
publishing and believed that the setting up of subject plans was unnecessary.
He was said to be opposed to the planned supply of paper and wanted free buying
and selling. He was critical of the quality of books being published. Those
who denounced him recognized that there were still problems in the industry,
such as overstocking and shortages, but they claimed that great advances had
been made through planning. [10]

Volume of Publishing

Together with the reorganization of the publishing industry there was a
sharp rise in the number of titles published--from 12,153 in 1950 to 30,196 in
1956--and an even more marked rise in the number of copies of publications
printed, owing to the growth in size of editions. The peak was reached in the
number of titles published in 1959; since then there has been a steady decline
to an estimated 5,180 titles published in 1964. We do not have any information
on the number of copies printed during recent years, but, according to the
observations of recent travelers in China who observed bookstore conditions,

the shelves were more full in early 1964 than they had been for some time.
From this we may infer that lately there has been an increase in the number
of copies printed that has more than offset the decline in the number of different titles printed. It is noteworthy that the present number of different
books being printed is only one-half of that for 1936, the last "normal" year
before the Sino-Japanese incident.

TABLE 6. *Number of Books and Copies*
Printed in China, 1936-1964

Year	Hsin hua pan yüeh k'an	Ch'üan kuo ts'ung shu mu	Ch'üan kuo hsin shu mu	Number of Copies
1936	9,438			178,000,000
1950	12,153			274,633,000
1951	18,300			703,304,000
1952	13,970			788,744,000
1953	18,384			754,519,000
1954	19,177	7,517		939,692,000
1955	22,538	10,750		1,079,574,000
1956	30,196	16,612		1,786,435,000
1957		15,584	9,666	
1958		26,414	15,112	
1959 (Estimate)			19,110	
1960 (Estimate)			15,618	
1962 (Estimate)			9,928	
1963			6,598	
1964 (Estimate)			5,180	

Sources: Second and fifth columns, Hsin hua pan yüeh k'an (New China Semi-
monthly no. 115, Sept. 1957, p. 82. Presumably these figures include all publications in addition to books.
Third and fourth columns, Ch'üan kuo ts'ung shu mu and Ch'üan kuo
hsin shu mu, respectively. Books only have been counted.

The figures given in Table 6 have been drawn from three different sources.
The slight overlapping of years covered by the three sources makes it possible
to compare the three different sets of figures and to note their discrepancies.

The Publishing House

(a) Publication planning. Planning in publishing is by no means new. Publishing houses are able to estimate their anticipated income from the sale of backlist materials; in countries where there is a practice of publishing in series, and where publishing periodicals in the same house is common, these ventures also have been found to give elements of stability to the house's projected income. Against these projections of estimated income the publishing house develops its future publication program. In China, the regulations mentioned earlier require this planning on a formal quarterly and annual basis from the publishing houses.

The plans that are made are evidently detailed ones. The People's Literary Press, for example, announced that it would publish classical and modern Chinese literary works and that popular reading materials on classical literature would require over 20 per cent of the total volume of paper to be used by the house in 1957.[11] Also at the beginning of 1957, the Commercial Press announced plans to publish 200 books relating to classical literature and the cultural background of China. Works in foreign literature were to include 30 new titles and 80 reprints.[12] The People's Press decided to publish 938 classical and contemporary books by Chinese and foreign writers in 1958. The Shanghai People's Press planned to publish 347 books in 1958 and to increase its net profits from 370,000 yuan in 1957 to 550,000 yuan in 1958.[13]

(b) Editorial work. In 1956 there were 9,690 persons engaged in the publishing industry, and 3,730 of these were editors.[14] These editors were responsible for the publishing of 30,196 publications, or over 80 publications for each member of the editorial staff. Of the editors, only one-fifth could work on their own. The editorial staff is spread very thin indeed, and is under continuous pressure to employ new writers and new translators. The National Conference on Publication Work in 1958 called for 10 per cent of the books to be published each year to be by new writers.[15] In spite of an increase in output from 318 books in 1957 to 380 in 1958, the Shanghai People's Press planned to reduce its editorial staff from 45 to 30 in 1958. Inevitably, these conditions have been reflected in the poor quality of work noted from time to time.

(c) Printing. When large editions are printed, matrices may be made centrally, with the books and periodicals printed locally for distribution. This principle was applied to newspaper publication in 1955. The major periodical Hsüeh hsi (Study) was published at six centers in 1957, and each of the local printings was over 100,000 copies. A large Chinese edition of the works of Stalin was reprinted in Peking, Shanghai, Mukden, Chungking, Hankow, and other places. [16] The third volume of the <u>Selected Works of Mao Tse-tung</u> was similarly handled for its first printing, which was printed in Peking, Shanghai, and Changchun and distributed from these places. [17]

The National Printing Work Conference for Newspapers, Books, and Periodicals held by the Ministry of Culture in 1958 surveyed the work of the past nine years and discussed future plans. It proposed the establishment of a national printing network during the next three years. [18]

The period since 1949 has seen many changes in Chinese printing. Printing techniques have been much improved with the introduction of more modern machinery, and China has given proof of its ability to publish books at a high technical level of printing. Romanization for periodical and news-paper titles has been a general practice since early 1958. In many publica-tions, horizontal printing has replaced the traditional vertical printing arrange-ment of the Chinese characters.

The emergence of Peking as a major printing center in China is another post-1949 development. Its output in 1963 was claimed to be scores of times greater than it was in 1949. [19]

(d) <u>Supply of paper</u>. The consumption of paper is low in China. In 1956 it was one kilogram per capita, compared with 12.5 kilograms in the Soviet Union in 1955, and 68 kilograms in England in 1954. The publishing industry is an important consumer of paper, but it is only one among many, having to compete with other industrial needs, expanding education, and other social demands for writing and recording material. For example, it has been es-timated that at the end of 1956 the rural cooperatives alone would consume 72,000 tons of paper a year. [20]

The production of machine-made paper increased from 108,138 tons in 1949[21] to 1,700,000 tons in 1959. [22] However, a slump in paper output since then is evident from a statement in the Peking <u>Ta kung pao</u> that the total output of paper had "increased" to one million tons. It is not clear whether this fig-ure refers to actual output in 1961 or to planned output for 1962. In either case, it is clearly below the level for 1958 and 1959, and under these condi-tions paper shortage in China must be acute. [23]

(e) <u>Size of edition</u>. In Chinese publishing the size of edition is determined by the publishing house. Before 1949 the average edition size was
about 2,000 copies.[24] During the 1950's very large editions became quite
common. The Shanghai newspaper <u>Wen hui pao</u> in 1957 stated that over seven
million copies of the <u>Thirty Years of the Chinese Communist Party</u> had been
published since 1951.[25] The <u>Selected Works of Mao Tse-tung</u> and other
classics of Chinese Communism have been sold in large editions. A book
such as the <u>Thirty Years of the Chinese Communist Party</u> must have reached
the maximum limit for the market.

For the purpose of this study, the number of copies for all titles entered
in the January 1958 issues of the <u>Ch'üan kuo hsin shu mu</u> were studied. Three
very clear groups emerge. The first, constituting 72 per cent of the total
number of titles, included all books with an edition size of less than 4,000
copies. The total number of copies of this highly significant group of titles
was less than 7 per cent of the approximately 16 million copies noted in the
January issues. The second group was composed of titles with an edition size
of from 10,000 up to 60,000. There were 271 titles in this group, and they
included over 35 per cent of the total copies issued. The final group consisted
of 31 titles with edition sizes ranging from 100,000 to 400,000 and also 3 titles
with edition sizes of 500,000, 720,000, and 900,000. This third group accounted for 57 per cent of the total number of copies published.

(f) <u>Book prices</u>. The Ministry of Culture may decree price reductions,
which are usually specified in terms of subject areas. For example, in 1955
the Ministry announced a reduction of 11 per cent on books on politics and
current affairs, 9 per cent on books on popular science and other general
reading matter.[26] In 1958 there was another selective price reduction. Books
on Marxism and Leninism were to be reduced more, and there were bigger
reductions on modern literature than on classical literature. The 1958 reduction averaged 15 per cent.[27] Through this price-control mechanism, the
Ministry of Culture can direct the general subject emphasis of the industry by
making books in certain subject areas more expensive than those in others,
thereby dissuading publishing houses from publishing in these areas.

There did not appear to be a relation between the size of edition and
price in the January 1958 group of publications. As a rule, prices of local
publications were lower than those of materials published in Peking and

Shanghai. Most of the large editions of over 100,000 copies were priced at
.10 yuan or less a copy.

(g) Localization of publishing. In most countries publishing tends to
concentrate in the major urban area. Peking, which is China's second largest
urban area, has shown rapid growth in its publishing industry relative to
Shanghai, but Shanghai is probably still the most important book publication
center, and in 1958 it accounted for nearly half of the titles published in
China. In 1957 Peking had 40, or a little more than half, of the national publishing houses. [28]

Kinds of Materials Published

Table 7, which was compiled from the Ch'üan kuo ts'ung shu mu, shows
the broad subject classes for books published from 1954 through 1958. There
was an almost fourfold increase in the total number of books published, and,
as could be expected, almost every class showed a major increase. Two
classes showing an almost sixfold increase were (1) engineering and technology and (2) agriculture and animal husbandry.

Table 8 was compiled from issues of the Ch'üan kuo hsin shu mu for
May and October in 1962, 1963, and 1964. Engineering and technology and
agriculture still maintain their leading positions, followed, as in the earlier
period, by literature.

A study of the kinds of subject matter issued by publishing houses, as
given in the Ch'üan kuo hsin shu mu for 1964, shows no strict relationship
between the subject classes and the names of the houses. For example, the
Shanghai Education Press and the People's Education Press publish material
in the subjects of language, science, biology, and even metallurgy, in addition
to publishing textbooks. One house with no indication of a subject role in its
name, the Peking Press, published in almost all fields and published textbooks
as well. A great deal of textbook publishing was carried out by the local publishing houses.

Table 9 shows the development of textbook publishing from 1954 to 1963.
The figures for 1963 were selected because a sampling based on the 12 issues
of the Ch'üan kuo hsin shu mu available for 1964 might not have been representative, owing to the irregularity of publication of textbook material, with

Table 7. *Chinese Book Publication Divided by*
Subject Class, 1954-1958

Subject Class	1954	1955	1956	1957	1958
Marx, Engels, Lenin, Stalin, and Mao	64	61	59	53	159
Religion and philosophy	44	161	176	232	218
Social and political science	385	589	616	731	1,034
History	204	337	421	346	366
Economics and economic policy	868	1,249	1,846	1,031	2,118
National defense, military affairs	15	37	44	63	86
The state and judiciary power, jurisprudence	54	84	125	110	78
Culture and education	517	644	1,222	984	1,478
Language	148	164	191	262	429
Literature	1,392	2,007	3,117	2,851	5,302
Geography	100	173	230	229	181
Arts	359	601	703	643	1,212
Natural sciences	453	547	620	822	1,150
Medicine	300	389	552	634	930
Engineering and technology	1,156	1,671	2,380	2,736	6,152
Agriculture and animal husbandry	410	452	1,277	994	2,375
Reference works	47	72	58	85	65
Total	6,516	9,238	13,637	12,806	23,333

Source: Ch'üan kuo ts'ung shu mu, 1955-1959.

Books in minority and foreign languages, juvenile literature,
textbooks, and books for the blind have been excluded.

its high concentration at the beginning of the fall. With the major decline by
approximately three-quarters in the total publishing output between 1958 and
1963, it is noteworthy that textbook publication during the same period declined
only about one-half.

Two special publishing houses are set up for children's and young
people's publishing, but about half of this publishing is carried out by the local
publishing houses. The figures compiled from the Ch'üan kuo ts'ung shu mu
show a rise in this area from 247 books in 1954 to 882 in 1957. According

*Table 8. Chinese Book Publication Divided by
Subject Area, 1962-1964*

Subject Area	1962 May and October	1963 May and October	1964 May and October (Estimate)
Marx, Engels, Lenin, Stalin, and Mao; the Communist movement	8	20	22
Philosophy, religion, and atheism	9	6	9
History	47	34	24
Economics		31	35
Politics and social life, law	25	6	12
Culture and education	32	50	48
Arts and music	85	73	81
Language	16	20	34
Literature – Chinese	148	128	181
– Foreign	22	15	7
Science	30	48	37
Geology and geography	18	14	9
Biology	26	16	17
Medicine	33	35	35
Agriculture	97	31	37
Industry	2	4	49
– Power machinery	3		12
– Electrical machinery, radio, automation	37	30	26
– Mining	23	2	8
– Metallurgy	23	23	36
– Light industry, handicrafts	3	7	2
– Chemical engineering	41	14	5
– Construction and highway engineering	31	33	28
General reference	3	5	2
Literature for the blind		11	25
Minority-language publications (Other than textbooks)	105	52	33
Minority-language textbooks	114	44	17
Foreign-language publications	32	64	57
Juvenile literature	37	51	44
Textbooks	245	138	65
Total	1,296	1,005	997

Source: Ch'üan kuo hsin shu mu, May and October issues for 1962, 1963, and
1964. Figures for no. 20 of October 1964 doubled, since no. 21 not
available.

Table 9. *Textbook Publishing in the Chinese Language,*
1954-1963

Level of Textbook Material	1954	1955	1956	1957	1958	1963
Kindergarten						14
Primary	21	62	130	49	356	325
Junior secondary	6	25	83	117	368 ⎫	
					⎬	296
Senior secondary	23	44	53	16	188 ⎭	
Vocational secondary	21	37	68		108	
Agricultural secondary						8
Teachers' college	94	117	203	15	36	17
Correspondence teachers' college					24	
After-work education					169	106
Literacy education					96	
Deaf-mute education					10	
General teaching reference works	3	32	3			
Other textbooks		8	22			
Total	168	325	562	197	1,355	767

Source: Ch'üan kuo ts'ung shu mu, 1954-1958, and Ch'üan kuo hsin shu mu,
1963. Excludes textbooks published in minority languages.

to the issues of the Ch'üan kuo hsin shu mu for 1963, 357 books were published
for children and young people during 1963, and this reveals the strong emphasis that is being placed on this type of publication in China.

Another area of popular reading is the picture book. In April 1952 the
China Monthly Review stated that 28,000 picture books in more than 28 million
copies had been published in Shanghai in the previous 40 years. Picture books
were a more effective method of reaching the general public than the movies.
In Shanghai, more than 200,000 people read picture books each day, but movie
attendance was approximately 100,000. Picture-book stalls where these materials were usually rented numbered 459 in Mukden, with more than 50,000
readers. Hangchow had 347 rental stalls. The rental stalls were found to

contain much material considered distasteful by the Chinese Communists, and a great deal was removed. The China Monthly Review article described as "feudal" 80 per cent of the volumes for rent in Hangchow.[29] In the next ten years, 20,000 serial picture books in a total of 600 million copies were published, and this popular channel of communication was utilized by the Chinese Communists for portrayal of acceptable themes. These materials were extremely popular among peasants and school children.[30]

Nearly all of the materials on the Communist movement and Communism were published by the People's Press in Peking, but in the areas of social and political science, economics, history, philosophy, religion and atheism, publications are shared between the local publishing houses and national houses with very little specialization among the houses. The China Finance and Economics Press publishes in the field of economics, but its publications are also found in other related fields.

Physical education materials are published almost entirely by the People's Physical Culture Press, but materials on culture and education associated with physical education are published primarily by the local publishing houses.

The Chung Hua Book Company in Peking and Shanghai and the Commercial Press in Shanghai have maintained their long-standing interests in language, but over half of the materials in this field are published locally. In Chinese literature, such literary publishers as the Writers' Press and the People's Literature Press still enjoy prominence, but again, most of the publishing in this field is carried out by the local houses. Drama is published almost exclusively by the China Drama Press. Foreign literature also has no local generation, and is published to a large extent by the Writers' Press and People's Literature Press. Music is published almost exclusively by the Music Press in Peking.

Local Publishing

Local publishing has expanded greatly since 1950. In that year publishing houses were to be found in 11 major cities.[31] The January 1958 issues of the Ch'üan kuo hsin shu mu noted that in 1957 the 27 local publishing houses published 301 books, over one-quarter of the total number of books published

in the period covered. A great deal of the expansion in local publishing has
been due to efforts on the part of the Publications Administrative Bureau.
Following a local publishing house conference held in April 1956, local houses
were required to develop long-term publication plans in the area of popular
reading matter for the Chinese peasant,[32] and in 1957 the Ministry of Culture
requested that the provincial and municipal houses publish academic materials
by local authors as well as more popular materials.[33]

In May 1960, Ch'üan kuo hsin shu mu entries show that the number of
active local houses had increased to 33 and that these were responsible for
over 40 per cent of the total number of titles published. Table 5 (page 15)
shows that in 1964, 35 of the 82 active publishing houses were local houses,
and a check of the Ch'üan kuo hsin shu mu in early 1964 shows that approximately one-third of the total number of titles published was from the local
houses.

Minority Publishing

Another area of great expansion has been the publishing of books and
periodicals in the minority languages of China. This development has a dis-
tinct parallel in the similar Soviet policy of encouraging publication in minority languages. One of the first steps taken after 1949 was to establish the
Sinkiang People's Press, in 1951, for the purpose of translating and publishing books and periodicals for the minority peoples of Sinkiang. In the
first 12 months of its operation this house published over 1,730,000 copies
of books and issues of magazines,[34] including large numbers of school textbooks. It was not possible to reconcile press statements regarding the numbers of books published in minority languages with the number of items re-
corded in the Ch'üan kuo ts'ung shu mu. These latter are shown in Table 10.

The most important publishing house in this field is the Nationalities
Press in Peking, which was established in 1953 by the Nationalities Affairs
Commission and the Publications Administrative Bureau.[35] In a review of
this press's work during the past ten years, the Min tsu t'uan chieh (National
Unity) for January 1963[36] reported that 2,900 titles in 24,700,000 volumes,
and 1,900 periodical issues in 14,000,000 copies had been published. However, the function of this publishing house has been largely taken over by the

Table 10. Publishing in the Minority Languages, 1954-1964

Language	1954	1955	1956	1957	1958	1960 Estimate	1962 Estimate	1963	1964 Estimate
Korean	140	157	311	285	498	408	174	114	72
Mongol	143	217	285	295	266	144	360	170	84
Tibetan	55	59	128	143	168	360	54	80	44
Turki	74	89	115	144	111	48	192	146	46
Uighur	87	124	160	248	165	120	245	198	68
Other								17	8
Total	499	646	999	1,115	1,208	1,080	1,025	725	322

Sources: Ch'üan kuo ts'ung shu mu for 1954 to 1958, and Ch'üan kuo hsin shu mu for 1960 to 1964.

local publishing houses in Sinkiang, Inner Mongolia, Kwangsi, Tsinghai, Szechwan, and in the Yenpien Autonomous Chou. In 1964 only 12 per cent of the minority-language publication was carried out by the Nationalities Press, and its materials were almost entirely concerned with Communism and the Communist movement.

All publications in the minority languages exhibit certain similarities. They are strong in materials for political indoctrination of the minority peoples and in the areas of culture, education, and literature, but they do not show the strength in natural and applied science publications shown by Chinese-language publications.

In 1953 the sizes of the principal minority groups for whom publications were issued were as follows:

Mongol	1,462,956
Uighur	3,640,125
Tibetan	2,775,622
Korean	1,120,405
Turki	470,000
Total	9,469,108, or 1.2% of the total population of China.

It is noteworthy that in 1964 over 6 per cent of the total number of titles being published was for 1.2 per cent of the total population of China.

Science Publishing

The principal publisher for the natural and applied sciences has been the Science Press of the Chinese Academy of Sciences. It was established in 1954 and publishes materials of an academic character. The Science Press is also China's principal periodical publisher, issuing a wide range of journals in cooperation with learned societies. Its growth is shown in Table 11.

In the period up to 1961, 40 houses were established for issuing natural and applied science publications, most of them with a special responsibility in a special field of applied science. Of these houses, only 10 survived until 1964; the special responsibilities of the others have been assumed by the survivors. One of the most active of these surviving publishing houses is the China Industry Press.

Only two subjects in the applied and natural sciences show a high proportion of local publishing. These are agriculture and medicine. There is a specialist house for agriculture, the Agriculture Press, but almost all publishing in this field is carried out by the local houses. For publications in medicine there are two national houses, the Shanghai Health Press and the People's Health Press in Peking. Again, however, almost all the publications in this field are issued by local houses.

In the natural sciences, the Science Press is the leading house, but some work in this area is carried out by the Science Diffusion Press and the People's Education Press. The Science Press also publishes in the fields of metallurgy and biology. The educational aspect of publications in biology is important, and the two national education houses publish biological material. Medicine is also stressed, and the People's Health Press issues materials in this class.

The China Industry Press publishes in the fields of engineering, geology, mining, metallurgy, and construction. There are two specialized houses, the People's Transportation Press and the People's Railroad Press, which issue books in engineering and communications. The Defense Industry Press also publishes in most branches of engineering.

Table 11. *Development of the Science Press, 1954-1963*

Year	Number of Periodicals Published	Number of Translated Books Published	Number of Original Books Published	Total Books Published
1954	85	122	72	194
1956	75			
1957		205	125	330
1959		251	156	407
1962	40			
1963				183

Sources: 1954 Peking Kuang ming jih pao, April 27, 1954, translated in SCMP 805, p. 39.

1956 Peking NCNA May 19, 1956, translated in SCMP 1295, p. 12.

1957 Peking Kuang ming jih pao, Dec. 28, 1957, translated in SCMP 1691, p. 13.

1959 Hong Kong NCNA English Jan. 2, 1960, pp. 1-2.

1962 Jen min jih pao, Nov. 15, 1962, advertisement on p. 6.

1963 Ch'üan kuo hsin shu mu, issues for 1963.

Periodical Publishing

There were 550 daily newspapers, 154 weeklies, 46 ten-day periodicals, 54 fortnightlies, 303 monthlies, 4 quarterlies, and one annual published in China in 1921.[37] In the mid-thirties, 450 periodicals were registered with the Ministry of the Interior, of which 99 were from Shanghai; it is estimated that there were another 450 unregistered periodicals, making a total of 900. The Shanghai Year Book, quoted by Lin Yu Tang, indicates that there were 212 periodicals published in Shanghai in 1934. The Shanghai Magazines Company, a periodical jobber, listed 345 periodicals in its December 1935 list.[38] This level of periodical publishing activity is superior to that of 1964.

A study of the 1,730 periodicals listed in the Chinese Periodicals-International Holdings 1949-1960, the most complete statement we have of the present periodical situation in China, shows a rapid growth in the number of new periodicals appearing up to the end of 1958, when the total number reached a peak, which was followed by a falling off in 1959 and 1960.

A study was made of all periodical advertisements appearing in the Jen min jih pao during 1961. A total of 330 periodicals were advertised, and an additional 46 titles were noted. Twelve of these new periodicals commenced publication in 1960. This would bring the total number of periodicals published in China from 1949 to the end of 1961 to 1,776.

Unfortunately, our data are very incomplete. For 721 of the periodicals listed in Chinese Periodicals-International Holdings 1949-1960 we have no date of first issues, and quite obviously we have inadequate data on the number of periodicals that have ceased publication. The data we do have are tabulated in Table 12. The year 1959 was not only the first year of the falling off from the peak year of 1958 but was also the year showing the most mergers (15 out of a total of 24 in the list), most title changes (28 out of 48), and most periodicals ceasing publication (29 out of 34). The same year also showed the most increases in frequency of publication, and the most decreases, 30 and 22 respectively. The evidence that we have, together with the sharp restriction on export of periodicals imposed in September 1959, indicates that this year was a most critical one in the history of Chinese periodical publishing.

A study of the imprints of 601 periodicals listed in the International Union List of Communist Chinese Serials shows that nearly half were published in Peking, a small number in Shanghai, and the remainder by learned societies and institutions, except for a small number published by local presses. It must be noted that this list is strongly biased toward the sciences.

The Peking periodicals tended to be published by houses according to their subject-class specialization. Many of these journals and houses disappeared at the end of the fifties. Three houses played an important role: the Mechanical Engineering Press, which no longer appears as a book publisher; the People's Health Press; and, most important of all, the Science Press, which published nearly one-fifth of all titles in the union list. Except in the case of these three publishers, periodical publication could not have played a major role in the planning of publishing houses.

A study was also made of 227 Chinese periodicals published in March 1958 available in the United States. These included all periodicals microfilmed by the Union Research Institute in Hong Kong and all periodicals, mostly

TABLE 12. *Chinese Periodical Publishing, 1921-1964*

Year	(1) Known New Titles	(2) Number of Science Titles	(3) Total Number of Titles	(4) Total Number of Copies Published
1921			408	
1934			900	
1950	64		274	35,000,000
1951	36			
1952	28		356	204,200,000
1953	30		277	172,000,000
1954	156		304	204,390,000
1955	135		376	
1956	162 (70)		465 (420)	
1957	55			315,000,000
1958	222			
1959	54	709		
1961		(47)	(310)	
1962		(150)		

Sources: Column 1. Chinese Periodicals-International Holdings 1949-1960. Compiled from dates of first issue given. In many cases this is from the appropriate section of Ch'üan kuo ts'ung shu mu. Column 3, 1950 to 1956 also compiled from the same source. Data are incomplete, as dates of first issue of 721 periodicals not known; also numbers of titles which have ceased publication not known.

1921 Lin, Yu Tang. A History of the Press and Public Opinion in China. Shanghai, Kelly and Walsh, 1936, p. 124.

1934 Ibid., p. 152

1950 Ten great years, statistics of the economic and cultural achievements of the People's Republic of China, compiled by the State Statistical Bureau. Peking, Foreign Languages Press, 1960, p. 189.

1953 and 1954 Column 4. Peking Kuang ming jih pao, Sept. 23, 1955, p. 4.

1955 Column 3. Peking Kuang ming jih pao, Jan. 10, 1956, translated in SCMP 1215, p. 22.

1956 Column 1 and 3. Peking NCNA Jan. 19, 1956, translated in SCMP 1215, p. 22.

1959 Column 2. Rafikov, A. "In Chinese Libraries." Special Libraries, vol. 51, no. 10, Dec. 1960, p. 528.

1961 Compiled from advertisements in the Jen min jih pao.

1962 Compiled from advertisements in the Jen min jih pao and articles in the Kuang ming jih pao.

in the sciences, held in Xerox copy form in the Library of the Massachusetts Institute of Technology. These two groups of material are fairly representative of Chinese periodicals, including as they do a balanced number of scientific and general publications. In the colophon of nearly all Chinese periodicals at that time could be found a statement of the number of copies printed of the issue.

TABLE 13. *Distribution of 227 Chinese Periodicals by Number of Copies Published in March 1958*

Number of Copies Published	Number of Periodicals
less than 10,000	139
10-20,000	29
20-30,000	14
30-40,000	9
40-50,000	4
50-60,000	4
60-70,000	3
70-80,000	2
80-90,000	3
90-100,000	1
over 100,000	19
	227

Table 13 shows the distribution of this sample of periodicals by number of copies printed in March 1958. The 19 major periodicals, all with circulations of over 100,000, were directed at young people or were general or literary periodicals. At the other end of the scale were over half the periodicals, with

TABLE 14. *Distribution of 139 Small-Circulation Periodicals in March 1958*

Number of Copies Published	Number of Periodicals
less than 1,000	5
1,000-2,000	41
2,000-3,000	23
3,000-4,000	17
4,000-5,000	13
5,000-6,000	9
6,000-7,000	14
7,000-8,000	7
8,000-9,000	4
9,000-10,000	6
	139

circulations of less than 10,000. Table 14 carries the analysis further and shows the concentration of the small-circulation periodicals between 1,000 and 5,000. Nearly three-quarters of the periodicals with a circulation of less than 5,000 were university publications or periodicals of the "hsüeh-pao" ("acta") type, a group publishing the finest Chinese scientific papers.

A study of circulation sizes in 1960, also based on the information in colophons but limited to 69 periodicals available, showed no sudden drop in the circulation size at the end of 1959, a situation which might have been expected in that year. Some understanding of the official attitude toward subscriptions to periodicals is gained from a statement that appeared in the Chieh fang jih pao (Liberation Daily) in February 1953. It pointed out that circulation had exceeded expectations and that some subscribers would have to be suspended. Allotted copies would be mainly for libraries, propaganda bodies, and public reference offices.[39]

Some classification by function of science periodicals may be undertaken in different fields. The periodicals with the smallest circulation are the "...chin chan," those recording advances in a particular scientific field. They describe foreign scientific developments and are at the same high academic

level as the "...hsüeh pao" ("acta") series but have a circulation of a thousand copies or less. A "...tung pao" generally has a circulation some ten
times that of its related "...hsüeh pao" periodicals. Other types of periodicals are the "...kuai pao," or "express" reports, the "...i tsung," or translation journals, and the "...wen chai," or abstracts.

In spite of the major scientific and industrial development that has taken
place in China in the past 15 years, China is extremely weak in the number of
scientific periodicals it produces. Japan, which has many of the language
problems faced by China, had 2,241 scientific periodicals listed in the National
Diet Library's Directory of Japanese Scientific Periodicals 1962 at a time
when there were only 150 Chinese-language periodicals. As early as 1954, a
writer in the Jen min jih pao described the scientific periodicals available at
that time and deplored the fact that there was only one periodical for each
field. Much more space was needed to publish scientific papers.[40]

The present condition of periodical publishing is not clear. Most periodicals available to us for examination no longer give circulation-size information in the colophons. From the limited data available there are indications
of a drop in circulations. The Che hsüeh yen chiu (Philosophical Research)
declined from 65,070 copies issued in June 1960 to 26,023 in May 1963, but
rose to 37,295 in December 1964. The Ching chi yen chiu (Economic Research) fell from 30,250 in March 1960 to 24,203 copies in August 1963, but
rose to 27,649 in December 1964. The K'o hsüeh tung pao (Science Bulletin)
showed a slight rise in circulation but changed its frequency from semi-
monthly to monthly in January 1961. Its 1964 level of circulation was the same
as that of 1960. The Hsin hua pan yüeh k'an (New China Semi-monthly) re-
verted to monthly publication in January 1962. The Hung chi (Red Flag) had increased its circulation over the latter half of 1959 and in January 1965 had a
circulation of 1,363,276 copies, a number far in excess of the important
party periodical Hsüeh hsi (Study) at its height in the fifties. At the end of
1964, other journals, such as the Li shih yen chiu (Historical Research) and
Wen i pao (Literary Gazette), were matching the circulation they had in the
late fifties.

A very large proportion of the 150 scientific journals published in 1962
were "express" reports, abstract journals, and indexes. Of these 28 had been
started in 1958 by the Science Press, and the number increased to 57 in 1960.[41]

Over 30 of them were being received in 1963 by the National Diet Library. Altogether, the Diet Library was receiving over 100 periodicals in the natural and applied sciences.

References

1. Jen min jih pao, June 20, 1950, p. 1.

2. Jen min jih pao, Nov. 1, 1950, p. 3.

3. Peking NCNA Sept. 13, 1951, translated in SCMP 174, p. 6.

4. Peking NCNA Nov. 1, 1952, translated in SCMP 444, p. 19.

5. Jen min jih pao, June 20, 1950, p. 1.

6. Peking Kuang ming jih pao, Jan. 10, 1956, p. 1.

7. Ibid.

8. Peking Ta kung pao, Nov. 28, 1956, translated in SCMP 1436, p. 11.

9. Shanghai Ta kung pao, Jan. 6, 1952, translated in SCMP 265, p. 9.

10. Peking NCNA July 17, 1957, translated in SCMP 1591, p. 11.

11. Peking Kuang ming jih pao, Jan. 24, 1957, translated in SCMP 1474, p. 19.

12. Peking Kuang ming jih pao, Jan. 15, 1957, translated in SCMP 1463, p. 15.

13. Shanghai NCNA March 1, 1958, translated in SCMP 1728, p. 28.

14. Hsin kuan cha (New Observer), no. 18, Sept. 16, 1957, translated in Extracts from China Mainland Magazines (ECMM) 111, p. 10.

15. Shanghai NCNA English March 18, 1958, in SCMP 1737, p. 18.

16. Peking NCNA March 17, 1953, translated in SCMP 534, p. 4.

17. Peking NCNA April 9, 1953, translated in SCMP 548, p. 6.

18. Peking NCNA Sept. 19, 1958, translated in SCMP 1867, p. 18.

19. Hong Kong NCNA English Jan. 12, 1963, p. 1.

20. Peking Ta kung pao, Feb. 19, 1957, translated in SCMP 1497, p. 14.

21. Ibid., p. 13.

22. Jen min jih pao, Jan. 24, 1960, p. 2.

23. Peking Ta kung pao, Aug. 22, 1962, p. 2.

24. Handbook on People's China, Peking, Foreign Languages Press, 1957, p. 155.

25. Shanghai Wen hui pao, July 1, 1957, translated in SCMP 1574, p. 6.

26. Peking NCNA March 6, 1955, translated in SCMP 1001, p. 20.

27. Peking NCNA English July 9, 1958, in SCMP 1811, p. 18.

28. Peking Kuang ming jih pao, Feb. 18, 1957, translated in SCMP 1495, p. 15.

29. China Monthly Review, April 1952, in SCMP 310, pp. 34-35.

30. Peking NCNA English Nov. 16, 1960, in SCMP 2383, p. 20.

31. Jen min jih pao, June 20, 1950, p. 1.

32. Peking NCNA April 25, 1956, translated in SCMP 1284, p. 23.

33. Peking NCNA July 28, 1957, translated in SCMP 1587, p. 29.

34. Tihua NCNA July 4, 1952, translated in SCMP 369, p. 25.

35. Peking NCNA Jan. 15, 1953, translated in SCMP 493, p. 14.

36. Min tsu t'uan chieh, Jan. 1963, pp. 9-12, translated in Joint Publications Research Service (JPRS) 18597, p. 46.

37. Lin, Yu Tang. A History of the Press and Public Opinion in China. Shanghai, Kelly and Walsh, 1936, p. 124.

38. Ibid., p. 152.

39. Shanghai Chieh fang jih pao, Feb. 23, 1953, translated in SCMP 523, p. 11.

40. Jen min jih pao, Oct. 14, 1954, translated in SCMP 916, pp. 27-30.

41. Chinese Academy of Sciences. Institute of Scientific and Technical Information of China. Annotated list of scientific and technical periodicals, 1961.

CHAPTER 3

DISTRIBUTION

The distribution of publications is an essential and final part of the whole publishing process. Before 1949, with the "three-in-one" process, large publishers such as the Commercial Press and the Chung Hua Book Company were responsible for their own distribution. They distributed to their own branches, which in turn distributed to other bookstores. The branches also acted as bookstores for retail sales of their own company's publications. The bookstores distributed for all publishers.

In 1950, when the Hsin Hua Shu Tien was organized on a national basis, it operated 887 retail branches and 30 printing plants besides carrying out its publishing function.[1] In 1952 the publishing industry was reorganized and the distribution process separated from publishing. A joint distribution company was established by the Commercial Press, the Chung Hua Book Company, the San Lien Book Company, and other houses. The new company was called the China Book Distribution Company.[2] It had branches in Peking[3] and Shanghai.[4] The principal book distribution company, the Hsin Hua Shu Tien, divested itself of its publishing and printing operations and rapidly became the leading distribution channel in China. In 1952 it distributed 80 per cent of the books published in China and was also responsible for textbook distribution for primary and secondary schools.[5]

A similarly complete or near-complete control of book distribution through jobbers or wholesalers is a feature of Japanese and German publishing. British and American publishing also have jobbing or wholesaling firms, but their role is limited. In Japan almost all publications are distributed on consignment according to requests made by the leading wholesalers. The wholesalers determine the distribution pattern of each particular publication through set schedules.[6] In China three kinds of agreements between the publishing house and the distribution network are possible. The first provides that the publishing house contract for distribution with the Hsin Hua Shu Tien for all books after they are printed. The second permits direct distribution to retail outlets by the publishing house. The third arrangement provides for the Hsin Hua Shu Tien to contract to take 60 per cent of the copies printed, and to pay for the remaining 40 per cent of the books when they are sold. In all cases the publishing house has the responsibility of determining the size of the edition.[7] It is fairly clear from these arrangements that the Hsin Hua Shu Tien has the freedom to refuse publications offered to it by the publishing houses, and there must be an area of negotiation here between the houses and the distributor.

There are few indications of the system used to determine what quantities of each publication are to be distributed to retail bookstores. We do know of examples in which there have been allocations of important works to bookstores. Volume 2 of the Selected Works of Mao Tse-tung was distributed to the South China branch of the Hsin Hua Shu Tien in Canton on the basis of the quota sold of the first volume. A total of 10,468 copies were to be distributed to this branch for sale.[8] The preciseness of the figure suggests distribution based on a quota system. Advance subscriptions were taken for the first volume of the Selected Works: In Hankow, 17,500 people applied for subscriptions after the first distribution had been sold out.[9]

The problem of determining the correct size of edition has been a major one for publishing houses everywhere. Attendant problems are those of book shortages and of overstocking. Shortages of books are not too apparent; our attention is drawn to them only as a contrast to the too obvious effect of overstocking.

The most spectacular overstocking has occurred with materials intended for very extensive distribution. In 1956 the publications of the Popular Reading Press were particularly noted in the press for being overstocked. Seven of the titles this press published were overstocked to the extent of 2,600,000 copies.[10] Under the more straitened circumstances of the industry today, it is doubtful that such major overstocking could occur.

The reports of overstocking help us to understand the internal circulation of books after they have been distributed to bookstores. Since a high proportion, if not all, of the medium-sized and large bookstores are branches of the Hsin Hua Shu Tien, this company assumes responsibility for the unsold publications and provides for their regional warehousing. We have a reference to the warehouse of the Peking Circulation Department of the Hsin Hua Shu Tien.

The same account gives accumulated stock reports from other parts of China, and from this it is clear that there must be reporting of stocks inside the Hsin Hua Shu Tien.[11] Another reference to surplus stocks was made in noting that universities with large book-purchasing funds buy one to three copies of everything in the unsold stocks of the Hsin Hua Shu Tien.[12] Unsold stocks are disposed of through sale as wastepaper; here again the Hsin Hua Shu Tien appears to have the responsibility. We have little evidence of the reissue of unsold books as new editions, unless a report at the 1962 National Book Distribution Work Conference is such an indication. According to the report, as many as 80 million books regarded as unsalable by bookstores in 1961 were redistributed to other parts of China where they were required.[13]

The annual conference of branch managers of the Hsin Hua Shu Tien plays an important role in the operation of the distribution company. At the fourth conference, held in March 1958, the distribution objectives for the year were declared. Greater over-all circulation was discussed, as was the development of specific markets, such as those serving the rural reader, children, and the scientific community. The 1956 conference also discussed the transformation of private into Socialist distribution and the use of supply and marketing cooperatives in the countryside for distributing purposes.

The effectiveness of the distribution system is shown by the fact that a substantial proportion of contemporary Chinese material found in American libraries was published by the local houses. This indicates that the product of these houses is able to reach not only the national but also the international market.

Retail Distribution

At the end of 1956, the Hsin Hua Shu Tien had 3,359 branches, subbranches, and bookstands, and 20,000 rural supply and marketing cooperatives as agents.[14] This was a considerable increase over the 1,700 branches it had in 1954,[15] and the 887 it had in 1950.[16] The China Book Distribution Company, formed by the Commercial Press, the Chung Hua Book Company, the San Lien Book Company, and other houses, is no longer mentioned in the press after 1953. Presumably it was absorbed by the Hsin Hua Shu Tien. Similarly, the many thousands of private bookstores were probably absorbed by 1957.

It is very difficult indeed to evaluate the significance of the total number of bookstores unless they can be put into some meaningful grouping by size of business. If we may assume that the proportions observed in publication distribution in Japan might have any bearing on the situation in China, there would be at the most some 200 class "A" bookstores in China, located in large cities only, through which scientific and specialized publications would be available. This group would handle all edition sizes except perhaps the very small editions of less than 1,000, which would be restricted to an even more select group of bookstores or would have a special distribution of their own. It would certainly handle the key group of edition sizes up to 4,000 copies, which at the end of 1957 made up 65 per cent of the total number of titles distributed. The class "B" bookstores would probably number about 1,000 to 1,500 and would be found in medium-sized cities. They would not handle many publications with an edition size of less than 10,000 copies but would specialize in the medium-edition-size range of publications, which constitutes 35 per cent of the total number of titles distributed. Class "C" bookstores, stands, and so on would circulate publications with edition sizes mainly of over 100,000. This distribution pattern would coincide with the pattern of edition sizes established for China and with the general pattern of book distribution found in Japan and other countries.

Although we have no over-all description of the distribution process, we do have sketchy pictures of the situation in Peking. In 1954 the Hsin Hua Shu Tien owned 20 branch bookstores, had many stands in the public parks and universities, and had specialized bookstores for scientific and technical publications, the classics, periodicals, children's literature, and art publications. In addition, outside the Hsin Hua Shu Tien there were 220 large and small bookstores, and the Guozi Shudian, with a 10,000-title stock of books in Russian, English, German, French, and Japanese.[17] In 1963 there were 90 general bookstores and the specialized bookstores mentioned above. Over 20,000 titles were offered for sale, the largest bookstore having a stock of 5,500 titles.[18]

Direct Distribution

Direct distribution is an important supplement to the wholesale and retail distribution of books. Inevitably, wholesale and retail channels cannot provide complete coverage. When publications are noticed and required but are not available at the bookstores, readers needing them will often request them from the publisher. The Shanghai Postal Bookstore, established in 1955, was one of six stores in 1959 that delivered by mail books required by readers. The Shanghai Postal Bookstore distributed 1,900,000 books through the mails from 1955 to 1959 and in 1959 was sending out books at the rate of 2,000 a day. The sales increase of scientific and technical books was particularly noteworthy.[19] The latter fact is significant, because it is precisely this group of publications that is likely to suffer most within a system that would seem to limit the distribution of these publications, which usually appear in small editions, to a small number of bookstores in major cities.

In 1957 formal approval was given to the publishing houses to handle their own direct distribution through the mails,[20] and in 1963 the Hsin Hua Shu Tien further extended the mail-order system by setting up mail-order departments in its bookstores in 28 cities. The bookstores are responsible for mailing and packaging expenses.[21]

Secondhand Bookstores

Secondhand bookstores form an important supplementary channel to the retail trade in new books, providing a source through which books no longer in stock may still be obtained. The secondhand book trade is highly specialized, particularly in the field of classical Chinese literature.

The buying and selling of secondhand books is an area of private trading which must have been repugnant to the Chinese Communists. In the enthusiasm for the new knowledge being introduced into China, they had little sympathy for the trade, with its marked classical traditions. As a result, the trade suffered. For example, 46 secondhand dealers in Tientsin before 1949 had been reduced

to about 20 in 1956. The control of the trade in Tientsin was placed under the
Hsin Hua Shu Tien, which did not consider that the trade had a future.[22] In
the spring of 1956, owing to pressure for socialization, many of these dealers
turned to selling new publications or to other kinds of business and sold their
stock as wastepaper.

The present situation in the secondhand trade is not known. The demand
for the kind of materials handled is still strong, as is evidenced by the fact
that the Shanghai Classical and Secondhand Bookstore has a total stock of two
million volumes and a daily turnover of thousands of volumes.[23]

Rental Bookstores

Our information on China's rental bookstore system is neither complete
nor up-to-date. It is known that the rental bookstore was firmly established in
the major cities until 1958. Materials handled were of a popular nature, principally picture or comic books. In 1952 there were 200,000 readers of picture
books a day in Shanghai; in Mukden, with 459 rental bookstores, there were
50,000 readers a day. Hangchow had 347 rental stalls.

The materials available from the rental stalls were, in the main, repugnant to the Chinese Communists. Controls were instituted at an early date. In
February 1951, 65 per cent of the stock of the Shanghai rental stalls was removed. In Hangchow 80 per cent of the stock was found to be objectionable.[24]
In 1955 the State Council passed regulations controlling the rental of books and
periodicals.[25]

In spite of controls and of campaigns in 1955 and early 1956 to reform
the rental stalls, at the time of the Hundred Flowers campaign in 1957 books
that were officially objectionable were again put out for rent. One of these was
China's Destiny by Chiang Kai-shek, which appeared in Mukden. This kind of
material originated from old stocks and sales of old books as wastepaper.[26]

Periodical Distribution

The total number of periodicals being published in 1956 was 465, and the
total number of copies published in 1957 was 315 million. The distribution of

90 per cent of these publications was entrusted to the Chinese Post Office. [27]
In 1955 the post office was handling 81 per cent of its periodical distribution
through subscriptions and only 19 per cent through retail sales. The post
office distributed periodicals to branches of the Hsin Hua Shu Tien and had its
own system of periodical stands and salesmen. [28] In 1963, 2,100 different
newspapers and periodicals were distributed through the post office. This
total probably included non-Chinese titles. Over half of the subscribers were
in rural areas. [29] The Chinese Post Office has itself expanded considerably.
In 1960 it was claimed that the number of postal and telegraph offices in rural
areas had increased from about 670 in 1949 to 59,000 in 1960.

Lists of periodicals distributed through the post office are issued by the
post office, or they appear in periodicals and in the press. In 1960, 315 different periodical titles were advertised in the Jen min jih pao, 18 titles as
many as 24 times. The majority of these were general, popular, or literary
periodicals. Only 42 were in the natural and applied sciences: 7 in the natural
sciences, 10 in the social sciences, and 25 in the applied sciences. Subscriptions to periodicals may be placed in post offices throughout China, and the
minimum period for one is 3 months. The post office places primary emphasis
on subscriptions, but there is also a limited retail sales program. [30]

We have some information on the distribution of periodicals in Shanghai.
In 1956 the residents of Shanghai subscribed to 1,170 different newspapers and
periodicals published in China. [31] In 1956 the Shanghai Post Office established
3,000 periodical stands in factories, businesses, government offices, and
schools. [32]

In Peking the post office had 20 stands and subscription departments
which were listed in the 1960 telephone directory. [33] Eight of these were periodical subscription departments, one a foreign-language periodical subscription department. These constituted only a small proportion of the total number
of stands in Peking.

The Market for Books and Periodicals

In a study made of the book market in Japan, a definite relationship was
established between the "intellectual population" and the sale of books. [34]

"Intellectual population" was defined as that part of the population which has received or is receiving education at the level of the former Japanese high schools or above. The higher the intellectual content of the publication, the more closely was this relationship established. In the case of periodicals, the general popular periodical sold more widely in the urban areas than in the rural areas, but there was a trend toward its establishing a closer relationship with the population as a whole, rather than with only the small "intellectual" section of it. The more specialized periodicals tended to have approximately the same limited circulation as specialized books.

In China, this group in 1960 would have numbered approximately 625,000,[35] the majority of whom lived in urban areas.[36] To this figure should be added the 434,600 students in institutions of higher education in 1957-1958,[37] making a total over one million, a number comparable with that of the Japanese group. This group, less than 0.16 per cent of the total population of China, probably constitutes the core of the book-reading and specialized-periodical-reading public of China.

The importance of Peking and Shanghai as the principal book markets and publishing centers of China is readily understood, as these are also the principal urban areas. The population of Shanghai was over seven million in 1957; those of Peking and Tientsin were also over seven million. The population of the Canton and Hong Kong areas combined was nearly four and one-half million in the same year.

Some further pointers as to the relative size of the book markets in China can be found in the distribution pattern of the Selected Works of Mao Tse-tung. Of the first volume, 30,000 copies were sold in Shanghai on the first day, 12,000 in Tientsin, and 5,000 in Sian.[38] These ratios are in almost direct proportion to the ratios of population of these three places in the mid-fifties. Of the second volume, 10,468 copies were allotted to the Canton Hsin Hua Shu Tien in April 1952.[39] This allocation confirms the hypothesis that the distribution of this work was made in proportion to the population of these major cities.

Great efforts have been made to develop the rural market for publications. Materials have been specially printed in simple language for rural readers. In 1956, 58 per cent of the total Hsin Hua Shu Tien distribution of publications, or 818 million copies, was made to rural areas.

The market may be stimulated by newspaper advertisements placed by publishers or distributors. Radio broadcasts, exhibitions, and book lists are also used to promote new books. [40] The most important stimulation to sales, however, is provided by the network of bookstores in which books are displayed.

International Trade in Chinese Publications

Both the publications import and export trades of China are handled by the Guozi Shudian in Peking. We have already described how this organization has centralized the subscriptions to foreign periodicals. Table 15 shows that 236 foreign-language book titles were published in 1957. This number increased to 338 in 1958. In 1963 one United States importer of Chinese books in English listed 426 English titles in stock and 10 periodicals in English. The Guozi Shudian also offers books in Chinese through its outlets outside China. The same United States dealer offers 12 such books, 32 periodicals, and a Chinese-language newspaper.

It is obvious that China attaches much importance to its publications in foreign languages. In 1964 they amounted to nearly 10 per cent of the total number of different books published, and nearly half of them were in English, French, and Spanish. China must be one of the world's leading publishers in Esperanto, publishing over 40 books in that language in 1964.

One of the sharpest setbacks to the international trade in Chinese publications was felt in September 1959, when without warning almost the complete list of Chinese periodicals previously offered for subscription through the Hong Kong dealers was made unavailable. Out of 106 Chinese-language periodicals in the natural sciences, mathematics, physics, chemistry, applied technology, biology, medicine, meteorology, geology, and geography, only 7 were not banned for export. On the other hand, out of 130 Chinese-language periodicals in the fields of literature, language, the arts, and social sciences, 47, or over one-third, were not banned. In this group there was no clear indication of the reason for the ban, except that the larger-circulation periodicals were not affected. However, some small-circulation periodicals, such as Kao ku (Archeology), were not banned, while some medium-circulation periodicals, such as Ching chi yen chiu (Economic Research), were. All of

Table 15. *Book Publication in Foreign Languages, 1957-1964*

Language	1957	1958	1962 Estimate	1963	1964 Estimate
Arabic		3	6	18	12
Burmese	13	26		15	16
Dutch		1			
English	62	73	84	71	100
Esperanto				23	44
French	33	40	24	35	72
German	21	32	12	27	50
Gujarati		1			
Hindi				9	2
Indonesian	27	35	12	16	16
Italian				9	12
Japanese	10	23	6	17	36
Russian	24	17		22	10
Spanish	14	30	36	28	52
Thai	2		18	12	26
Urdu	1	1			
Vietnamese	21	24		20	20
Other		7		38	36
Total	228	313	198	360	504

Sources: Ch'üan kuo ts'ung shu mu for 1957 and 1958, and available issues of the Ch'üan kuo hsin shu mu for 1962, 1963, and 1964.

the small-circulation, university-published periodicals were banned.

Of the 43 Chinese-language periodicals offered for subscription through Hong Kong in 1963, there was only one scientific periodical. This was devoted to science popularization.

References

1. Jen min jih pao, June 20, 1950, p. 1.

2. Shanghai Ta kung pao, Jan. 6, 1952, translated in SCMP 265, p. 10.

3. Peking NCNA May 5, 1953, translated in SCMP 564 p. 2.

4. Shanghai Chieh fang jih pao, July 21, 1952, translated in SCMP 384, p. 15.

5. Peking NCNA July 26, 1953, translated in SCMP 626, p. 18.

6. Nunn, G. Raymond. Modern Japanese Book Publishing. University of Michigan, Center for Japanese Studies. Occasional Papers, no. 8, 1964, p. 74.

References (Continued)

7. Peking NCNA Aug. 21, 1957, translated in SCMP 1600, p. 12.

8. Hong Kong Wen hui pao, April 8, 1952, translated in SCMP 311 p. 24.

9. Peking NCNA Oct. 12, 1951, translated in SCMP 193, p. 13.

10. Peking Ta kung pao, Nov. 28, 1956, translated in SCMP 1436, p. 10.

11. Ibid.

12. Ibid.

13. Peking Kuang ming jih pao, June 16, 1962, p. 1.

14. Hsin kuan ch'a, no. 18, Sept. 16, 1957, translated in ECMM 111, p. 13.

15. Peking NCNA Sept. 28, 1954, translated in SCMP 898, p. 27.

16. Jen min jih pao, June 20, 1950, p. 1.

17. Peking NCNA July 30, 1954, translated in SCMP 863, p. 37.

18. Peking NCNA English, June 19, 1963, in SCMP 3005, p. 16.

19. Hong Kong NCNA English June 12, 1959.

20. Peking NCNA July 28, 1957, translated in SCMP 1587, p. 29.

21. Jen min jih pao, Aug. 12, 1963, translated in SCMP 3047, p. 11.

22. Jen min jih pao, May 27, 1956, p. 6.

23. Shanghai Wen hui pao, May 14, 1959, translated in SCMP 2024, p. 23.

24. China Monthly Review, April 1952, in SCMP 310, pp. 34-35.

25. Peking NCNA July 25, 1955, translated in SCMP 1102, pp. 7-8.

26. Shanghai Wen hui pao, Jan. 24, 1958, translated in SCMP 1707, p. 22.

27. Peking NCNA Sept. 27, 1954, translated in SCMP 897, p. 18.

28. Tientsin Ta kung pao, March 19, 1956, translated in SCMP 1263, pp. 4-6.

29. Peking NCNA English, May 8, 1963, in SCMP 2977, p. 14.

30. Scientific Periodicals in Communist China, Current Background (CB) no. 366, Nov. 3, 1955, pp. 17-18.

31. Ibid., p. 35.

32. Ibid., p. 35.

33. Pei-ching tien-hua hao-pu 1960 (Peking telephone directory 1960) translated in part in JPRS 10684, Oct. 24, 1961, p. 1-20.

34. Nunn, Op. cit., p. 78.

35. Orleans, Op. cit., p. 127.

36. Orleans, Op. cit., p. 126.

37. Orleans, Op. cit., p. 68.

38. Peking NCNA Oct. 12, 1951, translated in SCMP 193, p. 13.

References (Continued)

39. Hong Kong Wen hui pao, April 8, 1952, translated in SCMP 311, p. 24.
40. Peking NCNA English, June 19, 1963, in SCMP 3005, p. 16.

CHAPTER 4

LIBRARIES

A National Library System

The publishing industry serves two principal purposes. First, it informs the individual reader who purchases a publication. Second, through libraries, it makes depositories of larger collections available for information. Although library purchases make up only a very small proportion of the total market for publications, their support is of considerable importance in the development of research.

It is clear that where a priority among purchasers must be decided, the Chinese Communists give preference to institutional or library needs over those of individuals. This may even be the case for periodicals with a major circulation, such as the Jen min chiao yü (People's Education) and the Hsin hua yüeh pao (New China Monthly).[1]

The National Library Coordination Act promulgated in November 1957 established joint programs among libraries, such as the conducting of surveys of resources and the compilation of union catalogues. In 1958 a national library system was established with two national libraries in Peking and Shanghai and nine local central libraries at Wuhan, Mukden, Nanking, Canton, Chengtu, Sian, Lanchow, Tientsin, and Harbin.[2] The system was established to undertake over-all planning, administer libraries of a scientific nature, develop cooperative procurement of foreign-language books, distribute books, and provide joint catalogues and photocopying services (Table 16). These projects are being conducted by the Council of Scientific Libraries, which is also determining the subject-matter scope of the major libraries. For example, the National Library of Peking will concentrate on the social sciences, while the Library of the Chinese Academy of Sciences will concentrate on the natural sciences and technology.

The Library of the Chinese Academy of Sciences, founded in 1954, was estimated to have over 1,750,000 volumes and its 113 special libraries over 4 million volumes. Its original holdings amounted to only 330,000 volumes.[3]

Table 16. Library Services in China

Type of Library	Number of Libraries	Library Holdings in Volumes	Number on Staff
Public libraries	400	31,090,000	3,714
Higher education institutions	225	33,400,000	3,568
Chinese Academy of Sciences	1,114	6,000,000 (1,750,000 in central library)	632 (232 in central library)
Rural reading rooms	182,960	16,610,000	
Trade union libraries	35,000	34,000,000	

Source: Peiching ta hsüeh hsüeh pao, jen wen k'o hsüeh, 1959, no. 4, translated in Union Research Service, vol. 19, no. 8 and no. 10, 1960.

The materials in the central and special libraries are selected by a committee of scientists, and over 200,000 publications are received annually.[4] The library has over 17,500 periodical titles, subscribing to 6,200 periodicals, of which 709 are Chinese journals and 527 are in the Russian language.[5] There are 5,316 library users, of which 62 per cent are scientists; 785 are institutional borrowers, including the branches of the Academy. In a ten-month period in 1958, 35,000 loans were made. Books are borrowed from other countries on interlibrary loan, and 453 such loans were made in 1957-1958.[6]

The special libraries of the Academy range in size from 10,000-20,000 up to 100,000 volumes. The Shanghai Branch Library of the Academy has over 500,000 volumes. The Academy has branches in Wuhan, Lanchow, and Canton. The Geological Library has 210,000 volumes.[7] The Central Library of the Academy issues a monthly bulletin announcing the acquisition of new foreign books, and its service department prepares bibliographical listings. In 10 months in 1958, 226 listings were issued.[8]

The major national library center is the National Library of Peking. It grew from 1,200,000 volumes in 1949 to 6,000,000 in 1961, becoming one of the world's largest libraries (Table 17). Founded in 1912, it built upon

Table 17. Growth of the National Library of Peking, 1931-1961

Year	Total Holdings in Volumes
1931	400,000
1949	1,200,000
1952	2,400,000
1955	Over 4,000,000
1957	4,800,000
1958	5,300,000
1959	5,600,000
1961	6,000,000

Sources: 1931 Ma, John T. "Chung kuo ta lu tu shu kuan chin shih ts'a lu (Notes on the recent development of libraries in mainland China), Hai wai lun t'an, vol. 2, no. 5 and no. 6, June and July 1961, p. 6.

1949 Shanghai Wen hui pao, Jan. 5, 1958, translated in SCMP 1693, p. 12.

1952 Peking NCNA March 20, 1953, translated in SCMP 536, p. 25.

1955 Peking NCNA June 13, 1955, translated in SCMP 1018, p. 7.

1957 Shanghai Wen hui pao, Jan. 5, 1958, translated in SCMP 1693, p. 12.

1958 Rafikov, A. "In Chinese Libraries." Special Libraries, vol. 51, no. 10, Dec. 1960, p. 529.

1959 Peking NCNA English Sept. 4, 1959, in SCMP 2094, pp. 16-17.

1961 Peking NCNA English Aug. 7, 1961, in SCMP 2557, p. 19.

former imperial collections dating back to the Southern Sung dynasty. Among its rare materials are 220,000 early books, half of which have been collected from private owners during the past 12 years. It is the national depository library for China and receives one copy of all Chinese publications within 3 days after printing.

The National Library shares with the Library of the Chinese Academy of Sciences principal control of international book exchange services and exchanges on behalf of 160 Chinese libraries. The extent of this exchange can be seen from the fact that nearly one-third of the 6,000 periodicals received in the library are obtained through exchange. It will be recalled that Table 1 (page 4) shows the extent of the exchanges conducted by the library for the period 1949 through 1961.

The National Library is the center of interlibrary cooperation inside China. Over 800 institutions throughout China are permitted to borrow from it, and in 1960 over 130,000 volumes were loaned.[9] It is also a local library center supporting library activities in or near Peking. The National Library maintains scores of mobile libraries in the Peking area[10] and nine large branches at institutions of higher learning. In 1958 it made nearly four and one-half million loans.[11]

The Shanghai City Library, established in 1952 on the basis of 2 existing collections, the Shanghai Newspaper and Periodical Library and the Library of Social Sciences, consists of 4 departments: social science, Chinese periodicals, natural and technical sciences, and guidance. It has a staff of 190 persons. The library has 3,600,000 volumes, 40,325 readers, and 2,365 institutional users. At the end of 1958 the library had established 2,400 "street" libraries, and the number of readers in these libraries reached one million.[12] These libraries may possibly have taken over the role of the former rental libraries that were popular in Shanghai in the early fifties.

Together with the Shanghai Branch of the Chinese Academy of Sciences, Ch'iao-t'ung Polytechnical Institute, Futan University, and the Shanghai First Medical Institute, the Shanghai Library established the Second All-China Central Library. This library acts as a center for university libraries, specialized institutes, technical research institutes, municipal industrial bureaus, and companies. Connections have been established with 75 major libraries in other parts of China.[13]

Until 1949 the Nanking Provincial Library was the Central Library for China and had at that time 500,000 books and periodicals. In 1949 the rare materials from this library were transferred to Taipei, where they formed the nucleus of the National Central Library. In China, the Nanking Library had increased to 2,600,000 volumes at the end of 1958. There were 400 periodicals from the Soviet Union. During recent years emphasis has been given to the natural sciences. Three million loans were made in 1958, and 10,000 books and periodicals were sent out on interlibrary loan to 300 libraries. The library issues a monthly bulletin listing the new foreign books acquired by libraries in Nanking, and it has compiled a union catalogue of foreign scientific literature in cooperation with 26 other libraries in China.

Another local Central Library was established in April 1958 to serve Kwantung, Kiangsi, Hunan, Fukien, Kweichow, and the Kwangsi Chuang Autonomous Region. Its collection includes all the books in six college and university libraries and one research library in Canton.

The Peking University Library is the largest of the university libraries, with 2,020,000 volumes, 91 staff members, and 10,000 student, faculty, and worker readers. An article in the Peking University journal, Peiching ta hsüeh hsüeh pao, reports that this university is the international exchange center for institutions of higher education and is actively exchanging publications with the Soviet Union and other countries. The article was written by students and faculty of the university, who may not have been aware of the international exchange arrangements that are generally believed to be handled through the Peking National Library and the Chinese Academy of Sciences. [14]

The Chinese People's University, formerly the North China University, had 60,000 volumes in its library in 1949; by 1959, this number had grown to 1,350,000 volumes. The library has compiled over 100 catalogues. [15] Twenty-eight other university libraries are listed in Mainland China Organizations in Science and Their Publications.

Thirty-one libraries have been established in the capital cities of the provinces, autonomous districts, and municipal districts under the provinces. Many of these libraries, such as those at Liaoning and Chungshan (Kwantung), have over one million books. Sixteen provincial libraries and 9 municipal libraries are also listed in Mainland China Organizations in Science and Their Publications. Below these libraries are 109 municipal libraries, 32 district libraries in urban areas, each under the direction of its local municipal library, and 673 hsien, or county, libraries located in the capital of each hsien. These, together with the 3 national central libraries and the local central libraries, form the national public library system. [16]

Catalogues, Classification, and Control

In the field of classification of library collections, the Decimal Classification of Liu Kuo-chün had been popular in China. It was replaced by a new system developed at the Chinese People's University. The first draft of the new system was developed in 1953, and a completed revised draft was issued in 1955. [17] The new classification was employed in the Ch'üan kuo ts'ung shu mu and, with the expansion in the subject scope of the materials to be classified, was expanded from 17 to 19 main sections. The classification is unusual in that it has a notation with a base of 1 to 19. This base is continued into the subdivisions, and until one is fully accustomed to it, it can be quite confusing. The following series is given as an example; the notation is in sequence:

17	Engineering and technology
171	Hydrotechnology
179	Transportation machinery
1710	Electrical engineering
1711	Telephone engineering
1713	Chemical industry
17131	Chemical engineering
171310	Fuel industry
171315	Paper industry

This classification system was most certainly devised to serve the general purposes of the regime, and it provides considerable room for the materials that have been published. In spite of its being a new scheme, the number of changes that have been made do not reflect favorably on its ability to accommodate new subjects. A new edition of the classification was published in 1962.

The second most important area of library activity has been the publishing of catalogues. Many of these have been cooperative ventures. An article appearing in the Ajiya keizai jumpō (Asia Economic Report) reported that 4,864 catalogues had been compiled by libraries between 1949 and 1958. The article lists 298 catalogues published during this period. [18] Publishing these catalogues serves to make research resources more widely known and to assist in the planned development of collections.

In addition to these catalogues of holdings, three important general bibliographical publications have been issued in China. The first of these is the Ch'üan kuo hsin shu mu, or National Catalogue of New Books, which was issued first on an annual basis in 1950, on a quarterly basis in 1951, semi-annually in 1952, annually in 1953, and monthly from 1954 until August 1958, when its frequency changed to three times a month. In recent years it has appeared as a semi-monthly. The August 1964 issues were published in editions of 12,860 and 12,850 copies, which gives some indication of the number of trade outlets and libraries that require this publication to carry on their day-to-day operations. The catalogue now gives the author, title, publisher, number of words, and price for each title listed. The materials are listed by subject, and each issue concludes with a number of sections for minority languages, foreign-language materials, textbooks, illustrated materials, and children's materials. The annual cumulation, the Ch'üan kuo ts'ung shu mu, or National Cumulative Catalogue of Books, was first issued in 1955, with a cumulation for publications issued from 1949 to 1954. The materials listed probably represent only those publications still in stock in 1955. The latest issue was published in 1959 and covered materials published in 1958.

The third major bibliography is the index to periodicals and newspapers, the Ch'üan kuo chu yao pao k'an tzu liao so yin, which was compiled by the Shanghai Newspaper and Periodical Library until 1959, then by the Shanghai Library. In January 1959, after 38 monthly issues, the index was divided into a philosophy and social science section, with a distribution of 5,030 copies for the February 1960 issue (the latest available issue), and natural science and technology section, with a distribution of 3,950 copies in November 1960. Each section indexed approximately 40 newspapers and 200 periodicals; items were arranged according to the Chinese People's University Library classification system.

References

1. Shanghai Chieh fang jih pao, Feb. 23, 1953, translated in SCMP 523, p. 11.

2. Peiching ta hsüeh hsüeh pao, jen wen k'o hsüeh, 1959, no. 4, translated in Union Research Service, vol. 19, no. 8 and no. 10, 1960, and Shanghai Wen hui pao, Jan. 5, 1958, translated in SCMP 1693, pp. 11-13.

References (Continued)

3. Rafikov, A. "In Chinese Libraries." Special Libraries, vol. 51, no. 10, Dec. 1960, p. 528.

4. Ibid.

5. Ibid.

6. Peiching ta hsüeh hsüeh pao, p. 142.

7. Ibid.

8. Rafikov, op. cit., p. 529.

9. Peking NCNA English, Aug. 7, 1961, in SCMP 2557, p. 19.

10. Peking NCNA, Dec. 27, 1953, translated in SCMP 716, pp. 11-12.

11. Rafikov, op. cit., p. 529.

12. Rafikov, op. cit., p. 531.

13. Shanghai Wen hui pao, March 22, 1959, translated in SCMP 1987, pp. 6-8.

14. Peiching ta hsüeh hsüeh pao, p. 141.

15. Ibid, p. 140.

16. Ibid, p. 140.

17. Liu, Kuo-chün, Tu shu kuan mu lu (Library Catalogues), Peiching, Kao teng chiao yü chü pan she, 1957, p. 232.

18. Ajiya keizai jumpō no. 417, Dec. 20, 1959, no. 421, Feb. 1, 1960, and no. 424, March 1, 1960, translated in JPRS 5244, Aug. 3, 1960.

CHAPTER 5

CONCLUSION

The Chinese publishing industry was refashioned to serve the purposes of the new state established in 1949. As a first step in this direction, ideological conformity was furthered by censoring all materials considered objectionable by the Chinese Communists. This censorship included even materials published after 1949. The contents of libraries — public, academic, and the more lowly though numerous rental libraries — were scrutinized, and materials removed. The stocks of distributors and publishing companies also underwent this process.

At the same time, the new ideology had to be established. This was done with the ready assistance of the Soviet Union. Many tens of millions of the Communist classics — the works of Marx, Engels, Lenin, and Stalin — were imported in Chinese editions from the Soviet Union or translated into Chinese and published in Peking and Shanghai. The same works were also translated into the minority languages, even into languages that had to be provided with written forms where none had previously existed. The less obvious areas where non-Communist thought might linger, such as the textbook, were also molded into the same ideological framework by the translation and publishing of thousands of Soviet textbooks.

Soviet scientific materials were translated to support the next phase, which involved the development of science and construction in a major effort to catch up with the Western countries. These trends are reflected in the proportion of Chinese translation of Russian works published through 1957, when such translation amounted to 38 per cent of the total number of publications issued. Translation from other languages, in spite of the role of English as the leading language of science, has accounted for not more than 5 per cent of the total publishing output since 1955.

Millions of books and periodicals were acquired by purchase and, to a much lesser extent, by gift or exchange from the Soviet Union. These were distributed to libraries, where they assisted in the development of major Russian collections. The teaching of Russian was increased, and during the mid-fifties 3,000 students were graduating each year as specialists in Russian.

The whole publishing industry was reorganized. Instead of being carried out by single firms, the functions of printing, publishing, and distribution were separated, and book distribution eventually was monopolized by the Hsin Hua Shu Tien. Periodicals were distributed for the most part through an expanded Chinese Post Office. Publishing houses were required to specialize in specified subject areas and submit plans showing the kinds of materials they proposed to publish. The number of houses was reduced to less than one hundred. In 1956 the concentration process was completed, with over half of the national output coming from seven major houses, while over half the houses published together less than 6 per cent of the total output of books. By 1958 the local publishing houses began to play an increasingly important role.

After 1959 a serious decline set in. In 1964 the rate of publishing placed China at the low level of approximately 5,000 titles a year, about half of the output in 1936. There appears to have been a similar decline in periodical publishing, where the levels also approximate those of 1935, except for a small number of large-circulation periodicals. It is difficult to hazard even a guess as to the reasons for this decline. The shortage of paper must have been responsible to some extent, and also, since printing requires fine adjustment, general engineering shortages could also have affected publishing.

There has been a corresponding development in the number of libraries and the creation of a national library system. In 1958, to mobilize library resources more effectively throughout China, considerable attention was paid to the development of union catalogues, particularly of foreign scientific materials. A new classification system was developed to accommodate the ideological emphases of Chinese Communism. The library system that was established would appear to have been adequate for service to research, and the needs of science were fully recognized.

The rapid growth of the publishing industry in China represented a triumph of contemporary China. But it has also come to represent a tragedy: the initial impetus could not be maintained, and levels of output sank back to the levels of the thirties and even below these. Under the present circumstances, Chinese development, particularly in science, rests on an extremely narrow foundation of documentation.

*But this is
1952 — many since.
Δs*

PROVISIONAL REGULATIONS GOVERNING THE CONTROL OF BOOK AND PERIODICAL PUBLISHING, PRINTING, AND DISTRIBUTION TRADES

Passed at the 116th Government Administration Council meeting on Dec. 21, 1952, and promulgated on Aug. 16, 1952.

Article 1   These regulations are enacted in pursuance of Articles 5, 41, and 49 of the Common Program of the Chinese People's Political Consultative Conference.

Article 2   The book and periodical publishing, printing, and distribution trades referred to in these Regulations include enterprises which, with fixed premises and installations, undertake the publication, printing, or distribution of books or periodicals.

Article 3   All enterprises that publish, print, or distribute books or periodicals, whether public undertakings, public-private joint undertakings, or private undertakings, whether specialized or subsidiary undertakings, shall be without exception subject to the control of these Regulations, unless otherwise stipulated by Government decree.

Article 4   All public and public-private enterprises that publish, print, or distribute books or periodicals shall apply to the local organs in charge of publication administration for permission to do business. They shall submit credentials issued by their direct superiors (Government organs, public bodies, or enterprises) and a letter of application stating their scope of business, conditions of installations (and if necessary, their business projects and other relevant papers).

Article 5   All private enterprises that publish, print, or distribute books or periodicals shall submit application for operation stating clearly their object of inauguration, their method of raising capital, their scope of business, conditions of installations (if necessary, also their business projects and

Appendix A

other relevant papers), and their names, and brief histories of the responsible persons. They shall file their application, which must be endorsed by two shops as guarantors, with the local organs in charge of publications administration for approval to do business.

Article 6　All public, public-private, or private enterprises that publish, print, or distribute books or periodicals, after obtaining permission to do business and possessing business permits, shall apply to the local industrial and commercial federation for registration by submitting the business permit.

Article 7　In case of alteration of organization, change of name, change of trade amalgamation, suspension or cessation of business, change of responsible persons in the enterprise, or change of personnel responsible for the execution of business, all enterprises that publish, print, or distribute books or periodicals shall apply to the (local) organs in charge of publication administration for approval. With regard to the sanction of suspension or cessation of business, the (local) organs in charge of publications administration shall consult the industrial and commercial federation.

Article 8　Those enterprises that publish books or periodicals shall observe the following stipulations:

1. They shall have a definite direction of specialization.
2. They shall set up an editorial board or appoint specially assigned editors.
3. They shall periodically compile projects on selection of subjects, editing projects, and publication projects, which shall be submitted to the local publication administration.
4. They shall give the number of the business permit on the copyright page in all publications.
5. They shall not print or distribute books or periodicals that violate the Common Program of the Chinese People's Political Consultative Conference or the decrees of the Government.

6. They shall not publish words or charts that disclose state secrets.

7. They shall not infringe upon the rights of other people's writings and publications.

8. The right of publishing decrees and documents of the People's Government at various levels shall belong to the People's Press at various levels or to publishers authorized by the People's Press. No other publishing enterprises shall be permitted to compile and print or reprint such decrees or documents.

9. Sample copies of all kinds of books and periodicals shall be sent upon publication to the publication administration at various levels and to state libraries. Relevant measures concerning this shall be enacted separately.

10. Publishers of periodicals shall apply separately to the (local) organs in charge of publications administration for registration. Relevant measures concerning this shall be enacted separately.

Article 9   Those enterprises that print books or periodicals shall observe the following stipulations:

1. They shall not undertake the printing of books or periodicals the publication of which is prohibited by express Government decrees.

2. They shall not undertake the printing of books or periodicals which violate the Common Program of the Chinese People's Political Consultative Committee or the decrees of the Government.

3. Before delivery they shall send to the local organs in charge of publication administration one copy each of the books or periodicals printed.

Article 10   Those enterprises that distribute books or periodicals shall observe the following stipulations:

1. They shall not sell books or periodicals the distribution of which is prohibited by express Government decree.

Appendix A

2. They shall not sell foreign books or periodicals which are illegally imported.

3. In providing a circulating supply [This probably refers to commercial lending libraries. Tr.] of books or periodicals they shall require an authorization from the local organs in charge of publications administration.

Article 11   Any violation of the stipulations given in Articles 8-10 shall be punished by warning or withdrawal of business permit, to be imposed by the (local) organs in charge of publications administration. In case of withdrawal of business permit, the local industrial and commercial federation shall be notified of the cancellation of registration.

Article 12   Under any of the following circumstances, enterprises that publish, print, or distribute books or periodicals shall have their business permits withdrawn by the (local) organs in charge of publications administration, whereupon the local industrial and commercial federation shall be notified to cancel their registration.

1. When it is discovered, after approval to do business has been granted, that there is serious false declaration of facts in their application, or that their scope of business has seriously exceeded the authorized limits.

2. When the name of another person is usurped in respect of writing, publishing, printing, or distribution.

3. When publication has been suspended without reasons for over six months.

Article 13   Detailed measures governing the application of the present regulations will be separately enacted by the Publications Administration of the Central People's Government.

Article 14   These regulations will be promulgated and put into effect by the Government Administration Council of the Central People's Government.

(Source: Peking NCNA Aug. 18, 1952, translated in SCMP 409.)

PROVISIONAL MEASURES GOVERNING THE
REGISTRATION OF PERIODICALS

Passed at the 116th Government Administration Council meeting on Dec. 21, 1952, and promulgated on Aug. 16, 1952.

Article 1   These measures are specially enacted in accordance with Subarticle 10 under Article 8 of the "Provisional Regulations Governing the Control of Books and Periodical Publishing, Printing, and Distribution Trades."

Article 2   Periodicals mentioned in these Measures refer to the following which are continually published in words or in pictures and are publicly distributed:

1. All periodicals other than newspapers.
2. All publications edited and distributed in the form of periodicals, although not published and distributed at regular intervals.
3. All periodicals published for circulation within Government organs, public bodies, army units, schools, and enterprises may also be registered in accordance with these Measures (if they wish to enjoy the privileges extended to newspapers and periodicals by the Post Office).

Article 3   Prior to the distribution of all kinds of periodicals, the principal person responsible for the publication shall write to the local organ in charge of publications administration for application forms for registration, which are to be truthfully filled out item by item and submitted as application for registration. The periodicals may then be allowed to be distributed only after the said application submitted by the (local) organs in charge of publications administration concerned has been approved by their superior authorities and the registration permit has been granted.

64

Article 4   Those periodicals which have been granted registration permit are subject to the "Provisional Regulations Governing the Control of Book and Periodical Publishing, Printing, and Distribution Trades" and furthermore are obliged to observe the following stipulations:

1. The number of the registration permit should be printed on every issue of the periodical (for publications on single sheets, it is to be placed under the name of the periodicals; for those in book form it is to be placed at the upper side near the back of the back cover).

2. On the copyright page, the name of the editor (chief editor) and the addresses of the editor and the printing and distribution offices shall be printed in every issue of the periodical.

3. Application for the renewal of registration permit or application for the extension of its validity shall be made one month in advance from date of expiration.

4. If the registration permit is lost, application for a supplementary permit must be filed immediately.

5. In the event of amalgamation, transfer of ownership, change of periodical's name, or alteration of publishers or editors, application must be made for alteration of registration.

6. When a decision to cease publication is reached, an application for annulment of registration must be made and the registration permit must be surrendered for cancellation.

Article 5   With regard to violation of these Measures, the (local) organs in charge of publications administration in various places may, with the authorization of their superior authorities, impose punishment by warning, suspension of publication for certain delay, or withdrawal of registration.

Article 6   After the promulgation of these Measures, all regulations concerning the registration of periodicals contained in various provisional or experimental measures on the registration of newspapers, periodical publications (magazines), and news agencies previously promulgated by the People's Government (Military Control Committee) at various places shall be abrogated.

Article 7   Detailed regulations governing the application of these measures will be separately enacted by the Publications Administration of the Central People's Government.

Article 8   The present measures shall be promulgated and put into effect by the Government Administration Council of the Central People's Government.

(Source: Peking NCNA Aug. '18, 1952, translated in SCMP 409.)

APPENDIX C

DIRECTORY OF CHINESE PUBLISHING HOUSES ACTIVE FROM 1949 THROUGH 1964

1. This list is not intended to be complete, but it does include the majority of publishing houses active since 1949 in China, including all the major ones. The output of the houses in this list has provided the basis for their grouping by size.

2. The houses have been divided into five categories, indicated by the letters AA, A, B, C, and D. Two periods have been used for the grouping, the first being from 1949 through 1957 (Table 18), and the second for 1958 through 1964 (Table 19). A separate category has been indicated for each part. For the first part, from 1949 through 1957, categories were determined by the value of output of each house. This was calculated from a sample made by selecting the first item from each page of the Ch'üan kuo ts'ung shu mu. The sample includes approximately one-eighteenth of the total output of books published each year. The items in the sample gave the total number of copies published and the selling price. By multiplying these together, and adding all items published by a particular house, the value of the output of the house was calculated.

TABLE 18. Categories of Publishing Houses, 1949-1957

Category	Value of Total Output in Yuan from 1949 Through 1957
AA	over 20,000,000
A	10-20,000,000
B	2-10,000,000
C	400,000-2,000,000
D	less than 400,000

Table 19. Determination of Categories of Publishing Houses, 1958-1964

Category	Number of Different Titles Published from 1958 Through 1964
AA	over 701
A	481-700
B	241-700
C	121-240
D	less than 120

Since comparable data on the numbers of copies published are not available for the period 1958 through 1964, the approximate size of publishing houses was estimated by the adding up of the total number of different books published by each house. The number of titles defining each group was adjusted so that there was some agreement between the two methods employed, and so that frequently a house which appeared in an AA or an A category for the first period would be found in a similar category for the second. An adjustment has been made for houses that were not active for the whole of each period.

Owing to lack of information, it has not been possible to locate all the publishing houses. Those in the provinces appear usually to be located in the provincial centers.

An hui jen min (Anhwei People's Press) 1952-1964 B   AA

An hui wen hua (Anhwei Culture Press) 1957   D

Chang an shu tien (Chang-an Book Company) 1954-1964 C   B

Chang chiang wen i (Chang Chiang Arts Press) 1955-1958 C D

Chang wang chou k'an she (Perspective Weekly Press) 1958 D
  Shang hai

Chao feng (Chao Feng Press) 1953-1955 C

Chao hua (Chao Hua Press) 1954-1955   C

Chao hua mei shu (Chao Hua Fine Arts Press) 1956-1964 D D

Che chiang jen min (Chekiang People's Press) 1951-1964   A
  Hang chou

Che chiang jen min mei shu (Chekiang People's Fine Arts Press) 1964 B

Ch'eng shih chien she (City Construction Press) 1956-1958 D D

Chi hsieh kung yeh (Engineering Industry Press) 1951-1960 A   AA
  Pei Ching Periodical publisher

Chi lin jen min (Kirin People's Press) 1956-1964 B   A

Chi pen chien she (Basic Construction Press) 1956-1960 D C

Chi shu piao chun (Technical Standards Press) 1964 AA

Chiang hsi chiao yü (Kiangsi Education Press) 1963   D

Chiang hsi jen min (Kiangsi People's Press) 1953-1964 C A
  Nan ch'ang

Chiang hsi tung tsu (Kiangsi Popular Press) 1952-1953 C

Chiang su jen min (Kiangsu People's Press) 1953-1964 B A
  Nan ching

Chiang su Su chou jen min (Kiangsu Suchou People's Press) 1960 B
  Su chou

Chiang su wen i (Kiangsu Arts Press) 1960-1964 C
  Nan ching

Chieh fang chün hua pao she (Liberation Army, Illustrated Press) 1956   D

Chieh fang chün wen i she (Liberation Army Arts Press) 1960-1963   D

Chieh fang she (Liberation Company Press) 1949-1950 A

Chien chu kung cheng (Construction Engineering Press) 1954-1960 D
  Pei ching   Periodical publisher

Chien chu ts'ai kung yeh (Construction Materials Industry Press) 1958 D
  Pei ching   Periodical publisher

Chien chu ts'ai liao (Construction Materials Press) 1956-1957   D

Chin shu (Metallurgy Press) 1958-1960 D   Pei ching
  Periodical publisher

Ching hai jen min (Tsinghai People's Press) 1957-1964 D B

Ching kung yeh (Light Industry Press) 1955-1960 Pei ching C
  Periodical publisher

  The object of this publishing house when it was established in 1954 was to
  issue books on technical, managerial, and other aspects of light industry.

Ch'ing nien (Youth Press) 1950-1951 D

  Merged with Kaiming Bookstore to form China Youth Press in 1951.

Chüan hsi jen min (Chuan Hsi People's Press) 1951-1952 D

Chüan pei jen min (Chuan Pei People's Press) 1952 D

Ch'un chung (Mass Press) 1951-1963 C   C

Chün feng wen i (Chun Feng Arts Press) 1963-1964   C

Ch'ün i tang (Ch'ün I Tang Press) 1963-1964   D

Ch'un lien (Ch'un Lien Press) 1954-1955 D

Ch'un ming (Ch'un Ming Press) 1955   D

Chung ching jen min (Chungking People's Press) 1954-1964 C A
Chung ching

Chung hua shu chü (Chung Hua Book Company) 1949-1964 B B
Shang hai, Pei ching

This long-established publishing house was charged in 1952 with the
publication of books in the fields of medicine, health, agriculture, and
the Russian language.

Chung i (Chinese Medical Press) 1951-1955 D

Chung kung yeh (Heavy Industry Press) 1950-1956 B

Chung kuo ch'ing nien (China Youth Press) 1951-1964 AA AA
Pei ching.

This publishing house was established through the merger of the Youth
Press and the Kaiming Bookstore. It had the responsibility of publishing
books for youth (teen-agers and children), and was under the direction
of the New Democratic Youth League Central Committee.

Chung kuo fu nü (China Women's Press) 1956 C

Chung kuo hsi chü (China Drama Press) 1957-1964 D AA
Pei ching

Chung kuo jen min (China People's Press) 1955 D

Chung kuo jen ta (China People's University Press) 1955-1958 C D
Pei ching

Published Marxist works.

Chung kuo kung yeh (China Industry Press) 1963-1964 AA
Pei ching

Chung kuo lin yeh (China Forestry Press) 1952-1960 C C
Pei ching   Periodical publisher

Chung kuo shao nien erh tung (China Young People's and Children's Press)
1963-1964   B

Chung kuo tien ying (China Cinema Press) 1956-1964 C B
Pei ching

This publishing house has the responsibility of publishing materials,
including translations, on motion-picture arts and techniques.

Chung kuo ts'ai ching ching chi (China Finance and Economics Press) 1964 C
Pei ching

See entry under Ts'ai ching ching chi

Chung nan hsin hua shutien (South China Hsin Hua Book Company) 1950 D

Chung nan jen min (South China People's Press) 1953-1954 C
Han kou

Chung nan wen i (South China Arts Press) 1953-1954 D

Chung wai (Chung Wai Press) 1954 D

Chung yang jen min (Central People's Press) 1954 D

Appendix C

Fa lu (Law Press) 1955-1963 C C Pei ching

Fang chih küng yeh (Textile Industry Press) 1952-1960 C Pei ching
   Periodical publisher

Fu chien jen min (Fukien People's Press) 1951-1964 C   AA

Fu chien jen min chiao yü (Fukien People's Education Press) 1964   D

Fu chien sheng (Fukien Province) 1957   C

Hei lung chiang chiao yü (Heilungkiang Education Press) 1963   D

Hei lung chiang jen min (Heilungkiang People's Press) 1955-1964   B

Hei lung chiang mei shu (Heilungkiang Arts Press) 1964 D

Hei lung chiang wen i (Heilungkiang Arts Press) 1956 D

Ho nan jen min (Honan People's Press) 1953-1964 B   AA

Ho pei jen min (Hopei People's Press) 1951-1960 B A
   Wu han

Ho pei jen min mei shu (Hopei People's Art Press) 1964 D

Ho pei lien ho (Hopei Union Press) 1950   D

Hsi nan ch'ing nien (Southwest China Youth Press) 1952 D

Hsi nan jen min (Southwest China People's Press) 1951 D

Hsi nan kung jen (Southwest China Workers' Press) 1951 D

Hsi pei hsin hua (Northwest China Hsin Hua Book Company) 1950 D

Hsi pei jen min (Northwest China People's Press) 1950 D

Hsin A (New Asia Press) 1951 D

Hsin chiang ch'ing nien (Sinkiang Youth Press) 1964 D

Hsin chiang jen min (Sinkiang People's Press) 1951-1964 C AA
   Established in 1951 to translate and publish books and periodicals
   for the national minorities in Sinkiang.

Hsin chih shih (New Knowledge Press) 1958 B C
   Shang hai

Hsin hua shu tien (Hsin Hua Book Company) 1949-1950 A

Hsin i (New Medical Press) 1955 D

Hsin mei shu (New Art Press) 1956 C

Hsin shih chieh (New World Press) 1963-1964 D   Pei ching

Hsin wen i (New Arts Press) 1950-1958 A B
   Shang hai

Hsin yun yüeh (New Music Press) 1953-1954 D

Hsu mu shou chi (Veterinary) 1958 D

Hsüeh hsi sheng huo (Learn Life Press) 1955 D

Hsüeh hsi ts'a chih she (Hsüeh Hsi Magazine Press) 1957-1958 D D
   Pei ching

Hu nan jen min (Hunan People's Press) 1951-1964 A AA

Hu nan k'o hsüeh chi shi (Hunan Science and Technology Press) 1960-1963 C

Hu nan tung tsu (Hunan Popular Press) 1951-1953 D

Hu pei jen min (Hupei People's Press) 1954-1964 B A   Wuhan

Hua hsüeh kung yeh (Chemical Industry Press) 1957-1960 B   Pei ching

Hua nan jen min (South China People's Press) 1952-1955 C Kuang chou

Hua pei jen min (North China People's Press) 1953-1954 D

Hua tung jen min (East China People's Press) 1951-1954 B Shang hai

Hung wen (Hung Wen Press) 1955 D

I shu (Arts Press) 1955-1957 D
    Pei ching

Jan liao kung yeh (Fuel Industry Press) 1951-1955 B

Jen min (People's Press) 1949-1964 AA AA Pei ching

Jen min chiao tung (People's Transportation Press) 1953-1964 B AA
    Pei ching Periodical publisher

Jen min chiao yü. (People's Education Press) 1952-1964 AA A Pei ching
    Periodical publisher

This has been one of the principal textbook publishers.

Jen min hua pao (People's Illustrated Press) 1951 D

Jen min jih pao (People's Daily Press) 1956-1964 C D   Pei ching

Jen min mei shu (People's Art Press) 1950-1964 C C   Pei ching
    Periodical publisher

Publishes arts publications, comic books, and propaganda materials.

Jen min tai yü (People's Physical Culture Press) 1951-1963 B B
    Pei ching

Jen min tieh tao (People's Railroad Press) 1952-1964 B A   Pei ching

Jen min wei sheng (People's Health Press) 1951-1964 A A   Pei ching
    Periodical publisher

Publishes in the field of medicine and health, including ancient Chinese
medical classics.

Jen min wen hsüeh (People's Literature Press) 1952-1964 A AA   Pei ching

Publishes classical and modern literary works, both Chinese and foreign
in translation.

Jen min yu tien (People's Posts and Telegraphs Press) 1953-1964 B Pei ching

Jih pua tung chi (Planning and Statistics Press) 1955 D

Kai ming shu tien (Kaiming Bookstore) 1949-1951 B
    Merged with Ch'ing nien to form Chung küo ch'ing nien

Kan nan jen min (South Kiangsi People's Press) 1960 D

Kan su jen min (Kansu People's Press) 1951-1964 C B

Kan su min ts'u (Kansu Minorities Press) 1964 C

Kao teng chiao yü (Higher Education Press) 1954-1960 AA A
   Pei ching

   This house was organized in 1954 to publish Soviet secondary and higher
   education texts in translation, together with similar texts written in China.

K'o hsüeh (Science Press) 1954-1964 B AA   Pei ching
   Periodical publisher

   Under the direction of the Academy of Sciences. Publishes academic
   materials in a wide range of subjects. The Science Press is also China's
   principal periodical publisher.

Ku'o hsüeh chi shu (Science and Technology Press) 1956-1964 B AA
   Pei ching Periodical publisher

K'o hsüeh kung ssu (Science Company) 1951-1956 C

K'o hsüeh pu chi (Science Diffusion Press) 1956-1964 C B
   Pei ching

K'o hsüeh yüan (Academy of Sciences) 1953-1954 C Pei ching

Ku chi (Classical Books Press) 1955-1956 D   Pei ching

Ku ten wen hsüeh (Classical Literature Press) 1955-1958 D B
   Shang hai

   Established for the reprinting of classical Chinese literary works.

Kuang hsi Chuang ts'u jen min (Kwangsi Chuang People's Press) 1960 C

Kuang hsi jen min (Kwangsi People's Press) 1953-1964 D B

Kuang ming (Kuang Ming Press) 1954 C

Kuan tung jen min (Kwantung People's Press) 1956-1964 D A
   Kuang chou

Kuan tung sheng (Kwantung Province Press) 1957 D

Kuei chou jen min (Kweichow People's Press) 1952-1963 C B

Kuei chou min ts'u (Kweichow Minorities Press) 1964 D

Kung jen (Workers Press) 1951-1960 A B   Pei ching

   Publishes popular literature.

Kuo chi mao i (International Trade Press) 1953 D

Kuo chi wen hu (International Culture Press) 1953 D

Kuo fang kung yeh (Defense Industry Press) 1955-1964 C B

Kuo kuang (Kuo Kuang Press) 1953-1955 D

Liao ning hua pao she (Liaoning Illustrated Press) 1957-1958 C D

Liao ning jen min (Liaoning People's Press) 1954-1964 B AA
   Shen yang (Mukden)

Liao ning mei shu (Liaoning Art Press) 1963 D

Lung men (Lung Men Press) 1951-1954 B

Man yang (Man Yang Press) 1949-1954 C

Mei tan kung yeh (Coal Industry Press) 1956-1960 C B Pei ching

Min ts'u (Nationalities Press) 1955-1964 D B Pei ching
    Periodical publisher

    Publishes materials in the minority languages. Established in 1953.

Nan fang tung ts'u (Southern Popular Press) 1952-1954 C

Nei men ku chiao yü (Inner Mongolia Education Press) 1964 D

Nei men ku jen min (Inner Mongolia People's Press) 1952-1964 C B

Ning hsia jen min (Ning sia People's Press) 1964 D

Nung yeh (Agriculture Press) 1960-1964 A Pei ching

Pai hua wen i (Colloquial Arts Press) 1960-1963 D

Pei ching (Peking Press) 1956-1964 C A Pei ching

Pei ching ta chung (Peking Masses Press) 1955-1956 C Pei ching

Pei ching tieh tao (Peking Railroad Press) 1957 D

Ping ming (Ping ming Press) 1950-1955 C

San lien shu tien (San Lien Book Company) 1949-1964 A B
    Pei ching

    Formed from the merger of the Sheng huo, the Tu shu, and Hsin chih
    publishing houses, for publications in the social sciences.

Sen lin kung yeh (Forest Industry Press) 1957-1958 D D

Shan hsi jen min (Shansi People's Press) 1952-1964 D A
    Tai yüan

Shan hsi jih pao (Shansi Daily Press) 1960 D

Shan tung hsin hua shu tien (Shantung Hsin Hua Book Company) 1949-1950 B

Shan tung jen min (Shantung People's Press) 1950-1964 B AA Chi nan

Shang chu kung ssu (Shanghai Publishing Company) 1951-1955 B

Shang hai chi tien (Shanghai Chi Tien Press) 1953-1955 D Shang hai

Shang hai chiao yü (Shanghai Education Press) 1960-1964 A Shang hai

Shang hai fo chiao shu tien (Shanghai Buddhist Bookstore) 1958 D
    Shang hai

Shang hai jen min (Shanghai People's Press) 1954-1964 B A Shang hai
    Publishes popular reading materials.

Shang hai jen min mei shu (Shanghai People's Art Press) 1954-1964 C B
    Shang hai

Shang hai k'o hsüeh chi shu (Shanghai Science and Technology Press) A
    1960-1964 Shang hai Periodical publisher

Shang hai wei sheng (Shanghai Health Press) 1956-1958 B B Shang hai

Shang hai wen hua (Shanghai Culture Press) 1955-1964 B A Shang hai

Appendix C

Shang hai wen i (Shanghai Arts Press) 1954-1964 C A Shang hai

Shang hai yin yüeh (Shanghai Music Press) 1951-1958 C D Shang hai

Shang ts'a (Shang Ts'a Press) 1950-1953 D

Shang wu yin shu kuan (Commercial Press) 1949-1964 B AA Shang hai
  The Commercial Press was given the responsibility of publishing books
  on languages, modern scientific works, and classical literature. Its
  former children's department was transferred to the Chung Hua Bookstore.

Shao nien erh t'ung (Young People's and Children's Press) 1958-1964 B
  Pei ching

Shen hsi jen min (Shensi People's Press) 1950-1964 C A Hsi an

Sheng feng (Sheng Feng Press) 1952-1955 C

Shih chieh (World Press) 1958-1960 C

Shih chieh chih shih (World Knowledge Press) 1950-1964 B C Pei ching

Shih p'in kung yeh (Food Industry Press) 1956-1958 D C

Shih tai (Epoch Press) 1950-1960 AA D Pei ching
  This publishing house was established by Tass and transferred to China.
  It has the responsibility of publishing materials on the Soviet Union.

Shih yu kung yeh (Petroleum Industry Press) 1956-1960 C C Pei ching
  Periodical publisher

Shou tu (Capital Press) 1952-1953 C

Shu mu shou i (Veterinary Press) 1950-1958 C C

Shui li (Water Conservation Press) 1956-1958 D D Pei ching

Shui li tien li (Water Conservation and Hydraulic Electricity Press) 1960 B
  Pei ching

Ssu chüan jen min (Szechwan People's Press) 1953-1964 AA Cheng tu

Ssu lien (Ssu Lien Press) 1954 C Shang hai

Sui yüan jen min (Suiyuan People's Press) 1953 D

Ta ch'ung (Masses Press) 1951-1954 D Pei ching

Ta tung (Ta Tung Press) 1952-1955

Ti chih (Geology Press) 1955-1960 B B Pei ching
  Periodical publisher

Ti tu (Cartography Press) 1953-1964 A AA

Tien chin jen min (Tientsin People's Press) 1956-1964 D B Tien chin

Tien chin mei shu (Tientsin Art Press) 1956-1964 D Tien chin

Tien chin tung ts'u (Tientsin Popular Press) 1951-1955 D Tien chin

Tien kung tu shu (Tien Kung Book Press) 1954 D

Tien li kung yeh (Electrical Industry Press) 1956-1958 B C

Tien shih chieh (Electrical World Press) 1954 D

Ts'a yün hsüan (Ts'a Yun Hsuan Press) 1964

Tsai ching ching chi (Financial and Economics Press) 1954-1963 B AA
    Pei ching Periodical publisher

    See Chung kuo tsai ching ching chi

Tse hui (Surveying Press) 1956-1960 C D Pei ching

Tso chia (Writers' Press) 1950-1964 B AA Shang hai and Pei ching

Tun huang wen i (Tunhuang Arts Press) 1960 C

Tung chi (Statistics Press) 1956-1958 C D Pei ching

Tung fang (Tung Fang Press) 1950-1954 D

Tung feng wen i (Tung Feng Arts Press) 1963 D

Tung hai wen hua (Tung Hai Culture Press) 1957 D

Tung hai wen i (Tung Hai Arts Press) 1957-1960

Tung li (Tung Li Press) 1955 D

Tung pei jen min (Northeast China People's Press) 1950-1954 C

Tung pei nung yeh (Northeast China Agriculture Press) 1950-1952 D

Tung pei tsai ching (Northeast China Finance Press) 1950-1954 C

Tung shu wen i (Tung Shu Arts Press) 1958 D

Tung ts'u tu wu (Popular Reading Press) 1952-1958 B D Pei ching

Tung ts'u wen i (Popular Arts Press) 1956 D Pei ching

Wai wen tu shu (Foreign Languages Press) 1964 AA AA Pei ching

Wen hsüeh ku chi (Literature Classics Press) 1955 C

Wen hua pu (Ministry of Culture) 1956 B Pei ching

Wen hua chiao yü (Cultural Education Press) 1955 D

Wen hua sheng huo (Cultural Life Press) 1949-1956 C

Wen kuang (Wen Kuang Press) 1952 D

Wen tzu kai ko (Character Reform Press) 1957-1960 D D Pei ching

Wen wu (Wen Wu Press) 1958-1964 D Pei ching

Wu han shui li (Wuhan Water Conservation Press) 1957 D

Wu han tung ts'u (Wuhan Popular Press) 1950-1952 C

Wu hsien tien (Radio Press) 1951-1954 D

Wu shih nien tai (Wu Shih Nien Tai Press) 1951-1954 B Pei ching

Yeh chin kung yeh (Metallurgical Industry Press) 1956-1960 C A
    Pei ching

Yen pien jen min (Yenpien People's Press) 1960-1964 B

Yin yüeh (Music Press) 1955-1964 B AA Pei ching

Yu tien pu (Ministry of Posts and Telegraphs) 1953 D Pei ching

Yun nan jen min (Yunnan People's Press) 1952-1964 B C

CHINESE EQUIVALENTS FOR NAMES OF PUBLISHERS IN TEXT

Agriculture Press	Nung yeh
Cartographic Press	Ti tu
China Drama Press	Chung kuo hsi chü
China Finance and Economics Press	Chung kuo tsai ching ching chi
China Industry Press	Chung kuo kung yeh
China Youth Press	Chung kuo ch'ing nien
Commercial Press	Shang wu yu shu kuan
Defense Industry Press	Kuo fang kung yeh
Engineering Industry Press	Chi hsieh kung yeh
Higher Education Press	Kao teng chiao yü
Mechanical Engineering Press	Chi hsieh kung yeh
Music Press	Yin yüeh
Nationalities Press	Min ts'u
Peking Press	Pei ching
People's Education Press	Jen min chiao yü
People's Health Press	Jen min wei sheng
People's Physical Education Press	Jen min tai yü
People's Press	Jen min
People's Railroad Press	Jen min tieh tao
People's Transportation Press	Jen min chiao tung
Popular Reading Press	Tung ts'u tu wu
Science Diffusion Press	K'o hsüeh chi shu
Science Press	K'o hsüeh
Shanghai People's Press	Shang hai jen min
Shanghai Education Press	Shang hai chiao yü
Sinkiang People's Press	Hsin chiang jen min

BIBLIOGRAPHY

Berberet, J. A. Science and technology in Communist China. Tempo
RM 60TMP-72, General Electric Co., 1960.

Chang, Chao and Cheng Te-ching. Tu shu fen lu fa (Classification of books)
Peiching, Jen min ta hsüeh tu shu kuan, 1962. 1249 p.

Chinese Academy of Sciences. Institute of Scientific and Technical Information of China. Annotated list of scientific and technical periodicals, 1961.

Contains information for periodicals published in 1960. Reprinted in
the United States in 1961.

Gould, Sidney H. Sciences in Communist China. Washington, American
Association for the Advancement of Science, 1961. 872 p.

Handbook on People's China. Peking. Foreign Languages Press, 1957. 235 p.

Houn, Franklin W. To change a nation. New York, Free Press of Glencoe,
1961. 250 p.

Hu, Chang-tu. China. Its people, its society, its culture. New Haven,
Human Relations Area Files Press, 1960. 610 p.

Liu, Kuo-chün and others. Tu shu kuan mu lu (Library catalogues) Peiching,
Kao teng chiao yü chu pan she, 1957. 375 p.

Massachusetts Institute of Technology. International Union List of Communist
Chinese serials, scientific, technical and medical, with selected social
science titles. Cambridge, Mass., 1963. 169 p.

Nunn, G. Raymond. Chinese publishing statistics, 1949-1959. Ann Arbor,
1961. 58 p.

— Chinese periodicals, international holdings, 1949-1960. Ann Arbor,
1961. 85 p.

— Chinese periodicals, international holdings, 1949-1960. indexes and
supplement. Ann Arbor, 1961. 107 p.

— "Modern Japanese Book Publishing." University of Michigan. Center
for Japanese Studies. Occasional Papers, August 1964, pp. 59-94.

Orleans, Leo A. Professional manpower and education in Communist China.
Washington, National Science Foundation, 1961. 260 p.

Peiching ta hsüeh hsüeh pao, jen wen k'o hsüeh. April 1959, translated in
Union Research Service, vol. 19, no. 8 and no. 10, April 26 and May 3, 1960.

Rafikov, A. "In Chinese Libraries." Special Libraries, vol. 51, no. 10,
Dec. 1960, pp. 527-532.

Ten great years, statistics of the economic and cultural achievements of the
People's Republic of China, compiled by the State Statistical Bureau.
Peking, Foreign Languages Press, 1960. 223 p.

U.S. Library of Congress. Air Information Division. Library Service Section.
List of Communist Chinese Scientific and Technical Periodicals, 1961.
63 p. (AID Report 61-21)

U. S. Library of Congress. Reference Department. Science Division.
<u>Chinese Scientific and Technical Serial Publications in the collections of
the Library of Congress.</u> Washington, 1955. 55 p.

U. S. Library of Congress. Science and Technology Division. <u>Mainland China
organizations of higher learning in science and technology and their
publications, a selected guide</u>. Washington, 1961. 103 p.

Young, G. B. W. <u>Some remarks on scientific achievement in Communist
China</u>. Santa Monica, RAND Corporation, 1962. 21 p. (Memorandum
RM-3077-PR)

INDEX